Oral History and Communities of Color

Oral History and Communities of Color

Edited by Teresa Barnett and Chon A. Noriega

UCLA Chicano Studies Research Center Press
Los Angeles
2013

CSRC Director: Chon A. Noriega
Senior Editor: Rebecca Frazier
Business Manager: Connie Heskett
Manuscript Editor: Catherine A. Sunshine

UCLA Chicano Studies Research Center
193 Haines Hall
Los Angeles, California 90095-1544
www.chicano.ucla.edu

Front cover: Chris Iijima, May 2005.

Library of Congress Cataloging-in-Publication Data
Oral history and communities of color / edited by Teresa Barnett and Chon A. Noriega.
    pages cm
Includes bibliographical references and index.
ISBN 978-0-89551-144-7 (pbk. : alk. paper)
1. Minorities--United States--Biography. 2. Minorities--United States--Interviews. 3. Oral history--Social aspects--United States. 4. United States--Ethnic relations--History. 5. United States--Race relations--History. I. Barnett, Teresa, author, editor of compilation. II. Noriega, Chon A., 1961- author, editor of compilation.
E184.A1O66 2013
305.800973--dc23
                                    2012044809
ISBN 978-0-89551-144-7 (paper)

♾ This book is printed on acid-free paper

This book is made possible in part with support from the UCLA Institute of American Cultures

Contents

Acknowledgments

This publication is the result of a collaboration between the UCLA Library's Center for Oral History Research and the UCLA Institute of American Cultures (IAC), which houses the four ethnic studies research centers: American Indian Studies Center (A(SC), Asian American Studies Center (AASC), Ralph J. Bunche Center for African American Studies (Bunche), and Chicano Studies Research Center (CSRC).

In 2006-07, the centers and institute hosted four visiting scholars who were doing oral history research related to the four ethnic studies research centers: Melissa Nelson (AISC), Irum Shiekh (AASC), Daniel Widener (Bunche), and Horacio Roque Ramirez (CSRC). Each visiting scholar taught a seminar related to his or her research project, and also participated in a faculty and librarian discussion group organized by the Center for Oral History Research.

The Institute of American Cultures provided grant support for this book. The following people were involved in setting up and implementing the collaboration: Shirley Hune, Teresa Barnett, Hanay Geiogamah, Darnell Hunt, Don Nakanishi, and Chon Noriega. Special thanks to Claudia Mitchell-Kernan.

Introduction

Chon A. Noriega and Teresa Barnett

This project has its origins in the paucity of oral history texts for classroom use that focus on communities of color.[1] Although one can easily argue that scholars working in ethnic studies are responsible for much of the oral history being done in the academy today, the standard manuals, works such as Valerie Yow's *Recording Oral History* and Donald Ritchie's *Doing Oral History*, are written by authors who do not work in communities of color and who present a view of oral history that is far removed from the projects that most students, and indeed faculty, are involved in. Similarly, the anthology that is most generally used in the classroom is Robert Perks's and Alistair Thomson's *Oral History Reader*, a volume that comes out of Britain and that, while it includes many excellent essays, has comparatively little on U.S. communities of color.[2]

The first purpose of this volume, then, is to assemble a collection of essays focused on communities of color—a collection that, on the level of content, reflects the kinds of oral history projects currently being carried out in most American communities and universities. At the same time, we do not intend these essays to be simply standard academic presentations that demonstrate the varied uses of oral history research. Instead, contributors use their research as a springboard to discuss methodological questions that are particularly salient in the communities with which they work; these questions touch on, for example, ethical considerations, the treatment of sensitive issues, and the value of giving back to the community.

The impetus for this volume was research carried out during the 2006-07 academic year, when the UCLA Library's Center for Oral History Research, together with the four ethnic studies research centers at UCLA, co-sponsored four visiting scholars who were engaged in studies that incorporated oral history research. While that year resulted in a wealth of wonderful classes and campus discussions, the five centers wanted to have a more tangible product, one that could have a lasting impact with regard to oral history research in communities of color. Thus, we envision this collection not as a comprehensive treatment of methodological issues but as a text that can be used in graduate or advanced undergraduate classes to supplement the standard oral history resources and that can also serve as a basic introduction for faculty and graduate students who are trying to start projects on their own, perhaps without the benefit of much oral history training.

The contributors come from several disciplines, including public health, media production, history, sociology, and anthropology. Their work contributes to specific ethnic studies areas—African American, American Indian, Asian American, Chicano/Latino, and Muslims in the United States—and it explores the intersections of race, ethnicity, gender, and sexuality. The contributors explore multiple dimensions of oral history not only as an aural, visual, and textual practice but also as a relationship that brings universities into dialogue with underserved communities. Several essays explore this relationship in the context of community studies, service learning, and other pedagogical models that situate learning and research in a community setting.

Our two final contributions turn the recorder, as it were, on the oral historians, subjecting them to the oral history process as a way of discussing—quite literally—their method for working in communities of color. Their ethos of being "present" and "giving" (noted by Horacio N. Roque Ramírez) and attentive to the dynamics "in the room" (advised by Karen Mary Davalos) constitutes a faith in communities of color as sites of knowledge production, one shared by all the contributors.

Not surprisingly, given the variety of approaches and concerns, the contributors understand what oral history is and does in somewhat different ways. These different understandings are in part a result of oral history's rich methodological traditions. To begin with the most basic definition of oral history—one taken from Don Ritchie's introductory manual *Doing Oral History*—oral history interviewing is the practice of "collect[ing] memories and personal commentaries of historical significance through recorded interviews."[3] What thus differentiates oral history from other forms of interviewing is that it is first and foremost a historical endeavor. Oral history is what Alessandro Portelli, in a play on the term *storytelling*, calls "history-telling"—a genre specifically designed to discover what individual experience means in historical terms.[4]

Most practitioners would also emphasize that the genre of oral history is not defined solely by its goal—historical knowledge—but by its particular way of eliciting that knowledge. Unlike many forms of qualitative interviewing, for example, the oral historian typically seeks a narrative, not just discrete answers to a set of questions. Oral historians are interested in how their subjects put together the history that they have lived through, and the interviewer's own interventions are largely aimed at amplifying the narrative that the interviewee creates—at drawing it out more thoroughly, clarifying it, encouraging the narrator to reflect on it, and so on. However much the course of the interview is and must be shaped by the interviewer, it is the interviewee who is the motor.

The narrator-centric nature of oral history interviewing has meant that "oral history" is frequently seen as synonymous with "life history." Obviously not every oral history narrates a complete life history, and, conversely, one can certainly do a life history interview as part of a therapeutic life review or other biographical project without any implication that that interview thereby has a historical purpose. And yet the equation of oral history and life history does identify something crucial about the oral history process. The fact is that oral history almost inevitably tends toward life history. That tendency may be expressed in the form of an exhaustive life narrative or in the simple fact that, even in a more focused interview, a good oral historian inevitably elicits background information that situates the topic at hand in the individual's life course. Oral historians aim for this expanded telling in deference to the basic historical principle of contextualization. A life history is a way of situating the telling, of getting behind the story and figuring out who is telling it and why. The emphasis on life history is also part and parcel of oral history's understanding that the history worth telling is not simply one more version of events; it is a story of how the historical plays out in an individual life, of how consciousness itself is inevitably implicated in history.

If we consider oral history as a methodological choice that involves, to a greater or lesser extent, these three components—a focus on history, an emphasis on narrator-driven accounts, a life history approach—then we can see that each of the contributions to this volume implicitly foregrounds particular aspects of the methodology. By most definitions, for example, the "talking circles" that Felicia Hodge describes are emphatically not oral history in that they are not concerned with expanding the historical record. And yet the emphasis on wide-ranging, narrator-generated stories, rather than the more limited, top-down questionnaires that one might more typically equate with medical research, draws this piece into dialogue with oral history and helps us think about how the process of oral history may also function as a means of clarification, narrator-driven social analysis, and empowerment. By focusing on oral history as life history, Karen Ishizuka and Robert Nakamura's interview with activist Chris Iijima, on the other hand, suggests how oral history inevitably demands an engagement with a specific individual and the trajectory of that individual's particular experience. In fact, each of the interview projects described in these pages parses the methodology in somewhat different ways and thus offers different possibilities for its use and applications. Collectively they demonstrate the range, flexibility, and subtlety of that varied set of practices we call oral history.

✦ ✦ ✦

In "Stories of the 'Sugar Illness': Using Talking Circles to Reveal Beliefs about Illness among American Indians Living with Diabetes," Felicia Hodge discusses the implementation of "talking circles" as part of a three-phase program designed to educate Sioux tribes about type 2 diabetes, "the sugar illness," and empower their members to manage the disease. Her study, the only one in this anthology not based in the social sciences, reveals how applying methodologies derived from oral history in this way was able to foster a healing dialogue within these communities and, ultimately, improve public health.

In 1998 the UCLA Center for American Indian/Indigenous Research and Education (CAIIRE) received a five-year grant from the National Institute of Nursing Research to develop and test an intervention program to reduce the prevalence of diabetes among adult Indians on four Sioux reservations located across southern South Dakota and northern Nebraska. The project had three phases: the implementation of eight talking circles that focused on participants' experience with type 2 diabetes, a series of intensive educational session for small groups, and an examination of medical charts to validate diagnoses.

The talking circles, which allowed for the recollection and collection of personal stories about the illness, were especially revelatory and useful in empowering individuals to improve their health. Rather than imposing a one-on-one or an insider-outsider interview dynamic, the circles were executed as an open forum in which community members of all ages could speak whenever they desired about their experience with and memory of the illness in their families. Speaking was not required, and participants were welcome to simply sit and listen. Other efforts were made to equalize the social dynamics of the discussion: no person was allowed to dominate the discussion, there was no "head" seat, and a tribal spiritual leader was always present to help navigate highly emotional topics. In addition, participants could come and go as they pleased, and there was no imposed time limit (one session lasted ten hours). For a community in which the storytelling tradition is a "vitally important means of societal communication, transmitting the history and culture of a people," as Hodges notes, these dialogues created a safe, comfortable place in which to share stories, impart wisdom, and engage in personal reflection. The talking circles were designed to suit the natural rhythm and rituals of the group, something individual interviews, a more common oral history method, could not do.

The spread of type 2 diabetes in these communities is rooted in displacement: the forced relocations of tribes from their Native lands and the placement of children in federal boarding schools broke cultural, social, and culinary traditions as well as familial bonds. More specifically, food-gathering practices changed. No longer able to acquire sufficient food through hunting and fishing, community members were forced to base their diet on minimally nutritive, government-provided provisions, and their lifestyle became sedentary. Meanwhile, the children who were sent to boarding schools lost their sense of Native identity, which deeply damaged their self-esteem. While much of this was previously known, the talking circles helped reveal that "the damage to emotional health went hand in hand with damage to the physical health" of these communities, and they provided a route to finally easing the emotional pain caused by those forced separations generations ago.

The talking circles helped instigate the process of changing "stories of tragedy to stories of healing." As the author describes, "each member learns from the previous speaker, and the dialogue weaves a fabric of information, concerns, recommendations, history, lessons, and truths." Although the CAIIRE researchers put resources in place to enable the discussions and to audiotape and transcribe them, they stepped away from the storytelling to let that process take its own shape, one that best suited this particular group. Then, in the following "medical" phases of the program, the communities were able to see that the disease could be managed, if not eradicated, through monitoring, medication, and healthful dietary and lifestyle habits. The patient had to be willing to take steps to control the disease, but the talking circles helped undo emotional blocks to progress. The program also brought to light circumstances that hindered patients' efforts, such as having no place within the reservations to walk for exercise.

This study argues that oral history methodologies helped foster healing beyond what could have been achieved by imposing "outside" medical attention and advice. "No one ever asked us about our illness," one participant offered, a statement very similar to responses that Davalos received during her interviews in the largely Chicana/o Chicago neighborhood of Pilsen. By having a venue in which to comfortably share their stories and engage the "emotional work" of oral history—an aspect also discussed by Roque Ramirez, discussed below —these Sioux communities could finally begin to recover aspects of their physical and emotional health that had long ago been lost.

In *"See* What I'm Saying? Adding the Visual to Oral History," Karen L. Ishizuka and Robert A. Nakamura argue for the use of video when recording oral histories. Specifically, they argue for video recordings of people of color because there is value to "seeing" a story being told, especially insofar as "race is visual." The authors situate their work as producers within the academic discipline of what they term EthnoCommunications as well as the larger legacy of Third Cinema, which challenges Hollywood-style production in order to create visible stories of people outside dominant discourse. Ishizuka and Nakamura are committed to recording expressions of the Asian American experience, whether through documentaries, memorial videos, or, as discussed here, video life histories.

The authors' argument for video life histories is based on their experience videotaping Chris Iijima, a singer-songwriter and leader in the Asian American movement in the early 1970s. Iijima was fatally ill at the time of the taping and died only five months after the interview was conducted. Still, he became fully animated during the interview, revealing his legendary charisma and love of performing. The authors conclude that this video life history captured a more intimate and authentic portrayal of Iijima than would have been possible with an audio recording or a transcript.

Ishizuka and Nakamura call for video life histories to pick up where audio-only oral histories have left off (and, before audio recordings, dictated or diary-like accounts), especially because older generations are passing rapidly. The goals of these video recordings are not different from those of other oral history methodologies, but more is achieved, they say, by "adding visual evidence" that captures non-verbal communication as well as the subject's surroundings. (This is a more visual version of the type of attentiveness to the details "in the room" that Davalos encourages.) The authors see video as useful in the process of documenting the "complexity and richness of the lived experience within intersecting dimensions of person's life." They note that people are not "audio-only communicators": the entire body communicates, not just the mouth.

Video life history offers people of color the opportunity to be "seen." After all, "race is visual," and in the realm of EthnoCommunications and beyond, visibility is the fundamental goal. There is a need, the authors say, for "griots of consciousness," a role in which they place themselves. Ultimately, the primary data collected in video life histories leads to secondary analysis and seeing "ourselves as we are." This is part of a political "inside-out" dynamic that the authors subscribe to: they are members of the community they wish to more widely present. The authors fully acknowledge that the interviewers are "in the driver's seat" as they do the pre-research, present the questions, organize the responses, and create the final product. But in this case, it is a decolonial arrangement, not the colonial, outsider versus insider relationship that defined early academic approaches to recording the stories of people of color.

The authors also speak to the value of modern digital technology in particular because, unlike film, it requires minimal lighting and equipment, and there is little sense of intrusion. Cameras are no longer the technology of the elite or, more cynically, the interrogator. As people grow ever more accustomed to being photographed and filmed in their daily lives, narrators are increasingly comfortable in front of the camera. Nevertheless, the sincerity and personal investment of the filmmaker to honor and broadcast personal stories goes a long way toward helping the narrator speak honestly on film. The camera also asserts the presence of an audience more prominently than a tape recorder can. In the case of Iijima, this served his life history well because it encouraged Iijima to present himself the way he had publically, as an artist and activist.

The authors acknowledge that there are some occasions when video is not appropriate, and they call for filmmakers to examine how they construct and control what they record on film and what is risked by their choices. For example, the authors chose to crop out Iijima's IV stand to keep the viewer's focus on the man, not his illness. In this regard, we must acknowledge video not as an absolute record, but as a tool that provides selective information about a subject.

It is also important to understand how different communication and recording formats are currently received, accessed, distributed, and valued, especially in the academy, which continues to privilege (and will more readily cite) print documents over video ones. The authors ask prospective video life historians to consider what impact they hope their work will make and to whom they intend to show it. Videotaped archival material may be less privileged in status, but it has the potential to be infinitely more powerful because of its populist appeal and presentation methods. "What a great amount of fun it was!" were Iijima's final words in his life history. While he was referring to the movement he led, the phrase also characterizes the experience of recording and watching his interview.

In "Not In Their Plans: Gentrification, Latina/os, and the Practice of Community Oral History," Nancy Raquel Mirabal describes an oral history research project she led that studied the negative consequences of the otherwise highly extolled gentrification of the Mission District in San Francisco. The study, which was conceived during an undergraduate classroom discussion in 1999 but was carried out, ultimately, over eight years, focused on the displacement of a Latina/o community from what had been a longstanding Latina/o neighborhood. By the project's end it had come to involve students, faculty, local activists, residents, shop-keepers, poets, and artists. Questions that guided the study focused on who was benefitting from the gentrification and who was being cast out and ignored because of it. Further, the study explored the implications and consequences of a community oral history among people of color vis-à-vis community change and development. Mirabal's essay also asks deeper questions about putting oral history into practice: In what ways can obtaining and engaging oral histories lead to political activism? Can and should oral history methodologies transition into activist scholarship? Mirabal elucidates how the "La Misión" project led her to rethink oral history interpretation, process, and practice.

The "La Misión" project was conceived in a matter of moments on the first day of teaching a Latina/o oral history class when many of the students expressed distress about the gentrification of the area and how it was displacing family and friends. The community-centered project that ensued utilized oral history to capture a multiplicity of voices con-nected to the change that was taking place. Rather than pursuing a life history method, the researchers divided interview subjects into groups and asked them questions based on certain predetermined categories such as "culture" or "business." In addition, the researchers examined public and media discourse about the changing locale, studied real estate policies, and analyzed census data that proved an outmigration or "loss" of African American and Latino/a populations from the city as a whole over the course of the Mission's redevelopment. This information provided context for the recorded testimonies.

Oral history methods, according to Mirabal, provided the tools to understanding what was "thought, felt, and experienced" by the community while the neighborhood underwent gentrification. Narrators offered a wide range of information about their experiences as the researchers explored the "the politics of language, authority, power, and space." Immigration and personal attachment to the area played a significant role in how the narrator experienced its change, which in turn pointed to a Latino community that was not at all monolithic. Observations made during walks became part of the record for both sides, as developers happily took interviewers on tours of their successes while the displaced pointed out what had been lost. That said, the narrators commonly expressed concern about who would have access to the stories they were telling and how they would be used.

Mirabal more pointedly discusses gentrification as "a process that restricted the movement of brown bodies in urban space" and how that process "replicated and reified" politics and policies that are embedded in definitions of property in the United States. Indeed, the project soon revealed not only the racialized nature of change in the Mission but also a systematic gentrification of San Francisco as a whole that was moving non-whites—especially Latina/os and African Americans—increasingly to the margin. This cultural transformation was determined by racialized definitions of space or, as Mirabal states, "the gendered, heteronormative, and masculinist meanings attached to spatial knowledge." She also points out that renaming neighborhoods, a common practice during gentrification, is the final punctuation mark in the process of erasing the past and differentiating between incoming (white) and outgoing (non-white) groups. In effect, those who control the language control the land, which suggests why oral history is vital.

The findings inspired the students and faculty to become activists for the displaced and those soon to be—in other words, to realize the social purpose of their work, beyond bearing witness to and documenting history, and to invest in the community. Mirabal notes that although this "divide between process and action" is typical of traditional oral history practice, in this case there was a growing impulse to build a bridge. Rather than "intervene and leave at will," as outside researchers tend to do, members of the research team got involved. "This was not a project that could be completed in the safety of one's university office," Mirabal says. "It was not an easy road to follow, but we had no choice." Expanding their definition of documentation to include action and participation was "both a disturbing and liberating prospect," she says. The research team decided to create an archive while simultaneously working toward influencing policy. Over the course of eight years, students and faculty wrote letters, made art, participated in city meetings, organized talks, and expanded educational and activist collaborations. All these actions revealed the numerous constructive possibilities for using oral histories within a community. "We learned to develop fluid, undefined spaces where different communities, including professors, students, artists, and members of nonprofit and activist organizations, could participate in producing knowledge and sharing authority," she says.

The author expresses her sense of obligation to report the "loss" of minority groups from urban areas, particularly in a culture in which a frontier discourse still celebrates developers and their whitewashing of "unsafe" non-white neighborhoods. History extends into the present, Mirabal says; it is not a closed conversation about a set of activities in the past. Her project shows how oral history can provide an alternate, activist discourse in the present.

In "It Wasn't a Sweet Life: Engaging Students in Oral History Interviewing across Race, Class, and Generations," Susan Rose describes the manifold results of a two-phase "college-community" oral history project conducted between Dickinson college students, faculty, and members of the African American community of Carlisle, Pennsylvania. The project applied oral history methods under the sociological framework of community studies, connecting students with the African American community that resided only blocks from the Dickenson campus. The positive outcomes included a documented history of the African American community in Carlisle that had not been a part of the town's "official history," and larger conversations about the dynamics and complexity of race relations in the town—in the present and the past—as personally experienced and understood not only by residents but also by the students. Ultimately, Rose asserts that to understand a community, researchers must look beyond demographic and economic data and specific historical events. More important are the dynamics of relationships, she says, "especially relationships between dominant and subordinate groups," which can illuminate how a past and present is perceived and how to affect change in the future. If pursued in this manner, oral history projects can serve as a history of the Other as well as "an inquiry into our relationships with one another."

Phase one of the "Smalltown" project occurred in 1989-90. The phase 2 "follow up" took place in 2001. In the first phase students and faculty worked in research teams with community members to collect multigenerational oral histories that revealed the ongoing development of the African American community in Carlisle. The collaboration ultimately improved relations between the two groups, who were prone to stereotyping each other, and revealed changes as well as continuity in race relations in the town over long and short periods of time. The second phase was similarly designed, but the greater diversity of students at Dickenson by this time provided dialogues, findings, and reactions from narrators and interviewers that were more complex.

For the faculty the project exemplified a method for incorporating important local issues into teaching and research while offering them opportunities to integrate themselves into the community. For the students, who served as researchers and historians for their own generation as well as the African American community, one of the key educational outcomes, says Rose, was that the project led to them not only to "see race" (for many whites, especially, for the first time) but then to "see beyond it." Most significantly, the project created greater understanding and empathy between the two groups.

Rose points out that the project empowered students as well as narrators, as both were seen, heard, and affected in the interview process. Although the interviews were directed only at community members, discussions in the classroom that preceded and followed the interviews helped students understand their own feelings of shame, guilt, or fear about race. Some of the interview questions were difficult for students to ask, but these sensitive personal and political questions activated the students' learning about themselves. The oral history method provided a path to self-reflection in the class as well as documents for the archive.

While Rose characterizes the "Smalltown" project in broad terms as a study of "change and continuity in race relations in twentieth-century small-town America," one of its main contributions is the careful delineation of the specific and nuanced dynamics taking place in Carlisle. Her essay suggests the need for more conversation between seemingly disparate local communities and offers oral history methodology as a way to help soften the divide. Many of the essays in this collection speak to the value of sameness between the interviewer and narrator, and it is notable that in this study Rose values the differences. The "Smalltown" project focused on a specific community, but it created the potential to serve many others by increasing the students' awareness of themselves and their place and power in the world.

In "Doing Oral Histories in the Shadow of 9/11: An Exploration of the Fears Surrounding Research," Irum Shiekh looks at how the racial prejudices and federal policies that developed in the wake of 9/11 have impacted—and most typically silenced—the storytelling of Muslims in the United States, especially those who have been detained by U.S. officials. The author, who uses oral histories as a way of educating the public about the inhumane treatment this group has suffered while under questioning or arrest, discusses the additional complications imposed by her own identity as a Pakistani Muslim and the racial profiling and fears of detention that she experienced after the George W. Bush administration declared a "War on Terror." The author's ethnic and religious background helped her build trust with many of her narrators, but it has also limited her ability to conduct her research and share her findings. "The constant awareness that people might see in me the face of an enemy affects all aspects of my research," she notes. Her voice, as well as the voices of those she interviews, is always in jeopardy of being silenced.

Shiekh speaks at length about the frustrations of conducting her research, including the access limitations that she endured while navigating a system marked by great antipathy toward detainees. She describes the numerous ways she tried not to draw attention to the fact that she was researching suspected terrorists. She also notes that "it was impossible to predict how individuals would respond" since the detention experience was so traumatic and fostered such distrust. Hesitations, refusals, and silence were not uncommon. Some narrators took years to agree to share their stories, which even then could be incomplete and unreliable.

Fortunately, many people did agree to speak, believing that justice could come from sharing their stories. And yet, even in those cases, both the interviewer and the interviewee engaged in a measure of self-censorship and took extra precautions to avoid the presentation of information that might be manipulated and might trigger further harassment. Although the story that is ultimately shared may not be entirely complete, the author states that the narrators' safety was her "paramount" consideration.

The author notes that her scholarship has sometimes been considered suspect; even publishers have expressed a concern that she may be sympathizing with her subjects because of her religion, regardless of her academic and other professional credentials. She states that we are living in a time of repression, when "free expression," which is essential to oral history research and all forms of scholarship, "can endanger personal safety." She does not intend to stop asking questions, however, because she believes that "the stories of the people arrested, detained, or deported on flimsy pretexts after 9/11 are stories that need to be told." Hers is ultimately an activist stance as, like many of her narrators, her desire to obtain justice has the strength to overpower her fears.

In her interview by Teresa Barnett and Chon A. Noriega, Karen Mary Davalos discusses how she has integrated oral history methodologies into her cultural anthropology scholarship. Davalos speaks primarily about her dissertation research in Chicago, where she used oral history methods to interview members of the Chicana/o working-class neighborhood of Pilsen. Davalos notes that she received no specific training in oral history during her doctoral studies at Yale and that she considers it "one of many methods" that can be useful to a cultural anthropologist. Moreover, courses in Chicano anthropology were not offered, and Davalos says that she learned about Chicano anthropology and the value of collaborative research while "going to conferences" and talking with her Latina/o and Chicana/o classmates "in the hallways."

At the time, in the late 1980s and early 1990s, research methodology in anthropology was moving from a colonial to an auto-ethnographic model, in which the interviewer identifies and considers himself or herself aligned with the same group he or she is interviewing. As a result, Davalos notes, "I just started to realize I had to figure out who I was before I could ask a question." Ultimately, she identified herself as a Mexicana/Chicana. Davalos says this has meant that she's walked an ill-defined line as an oral history researcher: she knew she wasn't an "objective" social scientist, "but I also didn't pretend I was the native."

Davalos raises several issues that pertain to the interviewer's subject position. She speaks at length about "adapting" herself to the narrator, of not being afraid to "take on a different persona" to develop a rapport with her subject. She "learned to eat meat again," for example, and played "the naïve younger woman." She talked about her Mexican grandmother, who wasn't formally educated, and the social significance of the way her grandmother spelled her name. All of these efforts were in service of "being a good interviewer." Her overarching rule in the auto-ethnographic model is "never … play the status card" by indicating any form of elitism or social difference relative to the narrator. Davalos talks about adopting the some of the habits of her narrators, such as riding the bus and wearing a uniform. Some of these choices were due to her own financial hardships, but she also "played" humble. She may have been a member of the working poor at the time, but her education gave her significant cultural capital, of which her interview subjects were very aware. Her challenge was to remain a non-elitist in their eyes, despite the certainty of her privileged future.

Davalos says that "unlike a good directed interview or open-ended interview, the oral history method ... lends itself to the reflective voice— the contemplative, the reconsidering—and that spills into the spiritual life." Indeed, she speaks extensively about the complexity of asking probing questions about religion and its importance. These questions must be framed as questions about faith, she says, because so many Latina/os, regardless of nationality, do not consider themselves "religious." This is particularly true for younger generations. Being "religious" evokes a certain set of practices and meanings that are not universal to Latina/os despite a universal identification with certain religious tropes and icons. Most critically, Davalos has found that most Latina/os do not depend on religious authority to define their faith in God. In her dissertation research, she says, it helped that she was not affiliated with one particular church or parish. Indeed, unlike Roque-Ramirez, Davalos actively explores ambiguities about religious practice in the Chicana/o community. "When you don't understand ... [Chicana/os'] relationship to the divine, you can't understand their daily experiences," she asserts. It is not possible to understand Mexican-origin people "without understanding their spirituality."

Davalos, like Mirabal, considers how a language of shared terms and concepts—in this case, regarding health, education, and religion—is essential to a successful interview because it fosters the type of "collaborative approach" that Davalos likes her interviews to take. Davalos suggests that this approach is the most ethical as well. Her procedure is to give the narrator the questions in advance. (Davalos calls this a "pre-interview," which often, she admits, "turned into the interview.") The narrator must then agree to the questions and be allowed to have some control over them. Anthropologists, she says, may not always be trained in oral history methods, but their willingness to let go of preconceived ideas about people serves them especially well when doing oral history research.

Staying flexible and open to surprise is an important element of oral history practice, as is holding the interview in the narrator's home. Asking questions about objects in the environment can elicit information that ranges far beyond that which would have been obtained from a set of predetermined questions. The interviewer, Davalos says, should pay attention "to the family's method of documenting" and to what is physically and psychically "in the room." While Davalos is not talking about video taping the interviews themselves (the focus of Ishizuka and Nakamura's work), she is suggesting that researchers think of themselves as a camera, taking in everything in view. Thus, she suggests looking at family photos or videos. Davalos goes one step further, however, and encourages interviewers to think in terms of not only who and what are in the frame but also who and what are not.

Davalos says that many of her Chicana narrators from the Pilsen neighborhood were in complete awe that someone would take an interest in their lives. They were both humbled and emboldened by her efforts, which advanced scholarship about and recognition of Chicana/o experiences. This raises the question of how we determine the value of life stories as told through oral histories. One answer that can be drawn from this interview is that if it is asked, it has value—for both parties.

Horacio N. Roque Ramirez has spent most of his professional career teaching and doing oral history research. His research has been primarily in the service of creating the first extensive examination of LGBT Latina/o history in the twentieth century, with a specific focus on San Francisco from 1960 through the 1990s. In his interview by Teresa Barnett, he discusses his commitment to the life history approach to oral history. He describes the limits and challenges of working with this method, and the extraordinary consequences as well. He also discusses his own subject position as an interviewer and how it has influenced his process and impacted his findings. As opposed to Mirabal, who contemplates oral history as a path into political activism, Roque Ramirez was and remains a political activist who uses oral history to engage not only the community but also the politics of the archive.

Like filmmakers Ishizuka and Nakamura, who have committed themselves to using oral history techniques self-reflexively—to record their own ethnic group "as we are"—Roque Ramirez has utilized oral history for a project in which his personal history as a gay man is directly embedded. In a choice that had significance for the direction of his research, he stopped repressing his sexuality at a time when the AIDS epidemic was still gripping the United States. He had a long-held interest in history and had developed a personal interest in the life stories of gay men in the Bay Area, but it was after taking a graduate seminar on immigration and oral history methodology at UC Berkeley that he realized an "archival impulse" to record these stories. He wanted to document the "bodies missing from the archive" at a time when gay men were dying rapidly and their voices were disappearing. He applied for a grant through Berkeley's Chicano/ Latino Policy Project to interview Latina/o HIV and AIDS patients, activists, and community educators.

He quickly came to prefer the life history method to the "well-orchestrated questionnaire," as it allows for more spontaneity, which could caption, in this case, "the pre-AIDS gay liberation zest" that he valued as part of the history he wanted to tell. This method also had other implications: it led him to see that he could not understand the role of the activists and community educators "if I didn't understand the role of AIDS and activism in their individual lives." This determination echoes Davalos's statement about spirituality in the Chicana/o community and how oral history methods can reveal key pieces to larger anthropological and historical questions.

Roque Ramirez admits that during his early interviews he did not ask the questions he would ask today, whereas he did ask questions he probably wouldn't today. He attributes this to his young age and his discomfort with his sexuality at the time. His later interviews were exchanges that were "definitely a lot more democratic" because he was more confident in delving into deeper issues about community, politics, and even sex. Still, being—and being seen as—*both* an insider (gay, Latino, bilingual) and an outsider (a Berkeley academic and too young to have been involved in "any of the internal drama that had happened years prior" in the LGBT community) proved a "good combination to get the project going."

The absence of documentation regarding this community has made Roque Ramirez insistent about obtaining names and naming places, a practice he instills in his students today. Narrators sometimes resist this request, however, and this became one of the many sensitive issues Roque Ramirez had to navigate while interviewing members of a marginalized community that had been further marginalized by a deadly disease. As a result, he adopted certain ethical practices specific to this project. These include honoring a narrator's request to change or hide names (although the narrative will always suffer, he notes), allowing the narrator to review his own interview transcript, and committing to fairness and accuracy in the transcription, analysis, and use of each life history whether the narrator is alive or dead. Indeed, Roque Ramirez poses questions about the "life" of an oral life history and the obligation of researchers to care for this information by transcribing, interpreting, and sharing it honestly, precisely, and with the amount of discretion the narrator requested.

Roque Ramirez makes the point that doing oral history is much harder and more involved than people realize. "Community projects take a lot of work," he says. "And faith—not the institutional kind, but the embodied kind." Oral history requires a commitment to the interview and the interviewee: "You have to be there, and you have to be present and you have to be giving." It is highly emotional work for both interviewer and narrator. In fact, he defines one aspect of his work as "creating a record of their feelings." At the same time, the oral historian needs to take his own experiences into account. Roque Ramirez admits that because he came from a "nonreligious" family and had no "shame" around religion himself, he "didn't pay enough attention" to religion in his interviews. But did he need to? His emphasis on building a "community's history" suggests not. And yet questions about limits and limitlessness ultimately define this discussion—from the extensive connections within each life history, to the increasing curiosity of the interviewer ("You get very hungry to know more of the history"), to recognizing intersecting communities in his and any oral history project. While his project illuminates the intersection of a queer community and Latina/o community, these kinds of intersections, he says, are "all over us," impacting us as researchers and historians. Because narrators experience "different levels of political engagement or expectations," their responses are similarly complex and multiple.

Like the other contributors to this volume, in the classroom Roque Ramirez stresses the point that academic work is not limited to the academy. It can also make a difference to a community. As these essays show, oral history research can be the opposite of an elitist or colonial exercise by including infinite voices and expanding the spaces where intersections of race, sexuality, gender, and other categories of identity can exist.

Notes

1. For an exception, see Charles E. Trimble, Barbara W. Sommer, and Mary Kay Quinlan, *The American Indian Oral History Manual: Making Many Voices Heard* (Walnut Creek, CA: Left Coast Press, 2008).

2. Valerie Raleigh Yow, *Recording Oral History: A Guide for the Humanities and Social Sciences*, second edition (Lanham, MD: Altamira Press, 2005); Donald A. Ritchie, *Doing Oral History*, second edition (New York: Oxford University Press, 2003); and Robert Perks and Alistair Thomson, *The Oral History Reader* (London: Routledge, 2006).

3. Ritchie, *Doing Oral History*, 19.

4. Alessandro Portelli, *The Battle of Valle Giulia: Oral History and the Art of Dialogue* (Madison: University of Wisconsin Press, 1997), 24.

Stories of the "Sugar Illness"

Using Talking Circles to Reveal Beliefs about Illness among American Indians Living with Diabetes

Felicia Schanche Hodge

A Lakota elder told this story:

> When I was growing up, my grandmother used to give [my] brothers and I buckets to go pick choke cherries and buffalo berries, wild grapes, sand cherries. We got our exercise while getting our traditional foods. Drying meat . . . deer meat. Picking and helping dry them. Cut them and put them on screens, then dry them that way or braid them.
>
> Also the corn, that was good.
>
> And squash too, that was good.
>
> Then the dried fruits with meat to make *wasna*, that was good.
>
> Using corn too, that was good.
>
> And of course we always had our bread.
>
> At one point in time the Lakota way of life was simple. But now technological advances have really complicated it to the point where we have to meet a time quota in many places. And in many times we are in a hurry and just grab something and eat here and there and we don't really take care of ourselves. If we would restore ourselves back to the simple Lakota way then we wouldn't have this stress [and death due to diabetes]. Our simple Lakota way kept us stress-free because we didn't have moral fault. Moral fault was brought to us by the society in which we live. If we wouldn't take that part of society we wouldn't be so stressed out, having the disease [diabetes] that we have today.
>
> The sugar illness that comes upon us has a calling card or a wake-up call. My wake-up call came. It was then that I realized the things I needed to do, to start taking care of my body.

This story comes from the Lakota Sioux of South Dakota. It is not a curing or a healing story. It is a story of tragedy—of a people facing disease and early death. In the view of the Lakota elder telling the story, the behaviors leading to the "sugar illness," type 2 diabetes, were adopted from others living in the larger society. The illness is taking from the Lakota community its very life and soul, first from the older and then from the younger members. The group has not lived with this sickness for very long. Ancestors can offer little help, as the illness came with the white men during grandparents' time. The storyteller, however, recognizes that tribal members can help themselves by going back to the ancestors' ways, the simple ways, and following what they learned from the ancestors.

This story is one of many told by the Sioux that transmit a lesson or a warning so that the tribe can live without having its parts taken away—the limbs, eyes, and lives lost to diabetes. The "sugar illness" is a story to be told to the right people, in the right time, so that the people can live.

The CAIIRE Research Project

In the late 1990s nurses from the Winnebago and Sioux tribes of Nebraska and South Dakota visited the Center for American Indian/Indigenous Research and Education (CAIIRE) office in Berkeley, California. They were concerned about the rising number of type 2 diabetes cases reported on their reservations. Surely, they reasoned, there must be some way to stop or slow the progression of diabetes among their people. The nurses offered to help collect data so that CAIIRE researchers could develop a culturally sensitive intervention to counteract the disease.

Type 2 diabetes, unheard of among American Indians before the 1900s, is now widespread on many reservations. It is particularly prevalent among Indians in the Northern Plains states.[1] The illness is often diagnosed in adult members of Indian communities and is now appearing even among children. The risk of developing type 2 diabetes is highest for people who are overweight, have a sedentary lifestyle, and have family members with the disease. When not properly managed, diabetes has devastating health consequences. Among many harmful effects, the illness can damage the small veins of the eye, leading to poor eyesight and eventually blindness; damage the kidneys, leading to kidney failure; and impair circulation, so that infection can result in the loss of toes and even limbs. In too many cases the person dies prematurely, usually from cardiovascular disease.

In 1998 the CAIIRE research center applied for and received a five-year grant from the National Institute of Nursing Research to develop and test an intervention to reduce the prevalence of diabetes among adult Indians on the Sioux reservations of Pine Ridge, Rosebud, Yankton, and Winnebago. These four reservations are located relatively close to one another in southern South Dakota and adjoining northern Nebraska. The project was designed to gather information on the cultural construction of diabetes among tribal members and then develop, implement, and test an adult education curriculum aimed at changing attitudes and behaviors related to the disease.

The project had three phases.[2] The first consisted of a series of eight "talking circles," two at each of the four reservations. Similar to focus groups, these circles provided guidance for the development of the intervention. Individuals with diabetes and their family members told stories about their experiences with the illness and the dietary habits associated with it. All the stories were audiotaped and then transcribed.

The second phase was the development and testing of the Diabetes Wellness Project, a series of intensive learning sessions in which small groups of adults with diabetes met once a week for twelve weeks. The curriculum incorporated culturally sensitive lessons on diabetes risks, on nutrition and exercise, and on empowerment strategies for overcoming diabetes. Participants took pre-tests and post-tests to measure their acquisition of knowledge and changes in their behavior and attitudes.

The third phase was the examination of participants' medical charts to validate the diagnosis of diabetes and identify co-morbid health conditions such as hypertension, cardiovascular disease, and obesity.

Of particular interest from an oral history standpoint is the first phase of this project, in which stories of health and illness were collected from members of the Northern Plains tribes.

Drawing on Storytelling Traditions: The Talking Circles

Storytelling is a traditional method of dialogue among all indigenous groups, taking place within families, peer groups, and communities. It is a vitally important means of societal communication, transmitting the history and culture of a people.[3] American Indian stories go beyond simple entertainment to affirm central ideas and values of the community.[4] Some stories use animal characters to demonstrate good and evil, while others highlight an ancestor who imparts wisdom in words. Many stories illustrate behaviors and their consequences (including illness) and encourage listeners to learn from these lessons. Personal reflection is paramount, for the listener must take ownership of his or her interpretation of the story. The storytellers have done their job if their listeners have accepted the story and have learned and grown from it.

The CAIIRE project drew on these indigenous storytelling traditions to create a safe, comfortable place for American Indian adults to share their stories of health and illness. Gatherings took the form of talking circles, group discussions in which all participants can speak and be heard.

American Indian nurses recruited participants and obtained consent from each person as required by institutional review boards at the University of California at Berkeley, the University of Minnesota, and Little Priest Tribal College on the Winnebago reservation. Although the project was administered at Berkeley and Minnesota, Little Priest College holds the institutional review board certification for the Winnebago tribes, so human subjects review and approval was required at each institution. In addition, each of the participating tribes provided a resolution of support from its tribal council.

Each talking circle dialogue starts with introductions, as group members situate themselves in time and geography. A woman might introduce herself as the "daughter of so-and-so." She might say she belongs to the "Nakota people, the Keepers of the Sacred Pipestone," or to one of the other two bands of Sioux, the Dakota and the Lakota. Even though some members of the group may already know each other, introductions are an expected way of presenting oneself in a formal and respectful manner.

Once the formalities are completed, the group begins tentatively and gently by discussing broad topics that are allowed to develop and grow. Members of the talking circle may choose to talk or to sit back and not talk; if they speak, they cannot aggressively take the floor and dominate the topic, for all voices must be heard and respected. No one is at the head of the table, and no one stands above another. Each member learns from the previous speaker, and the dialogue weaves a fabric of information, concerns, recommendations, history, lessons, and truths.

Tribal members came with family and friends to "testify" and tell their stories of the sugar illness. Mothers and fathers, aunts and uncles came with children, grandparents, and great-grandparents. When asked why they kept coming, one person explained, "No one ever asked us about our illness." One session lasted for ten hours. Doors were kept open and the tribal spiritual leader was called to assist in the session, as the stories were powerful and group members needed support to navigate emotional topics.

Stories of Ancestors

Stories of "those who came before us" establish the time and place for current tribal members' existence. The Sioux tribal website contains the following information on Sioux history:

> We came from the eastern woodlands (now called Minnesota and Canada). Seven Bands were a loose confederation of common ancestries call the Seven Council Fires. The word Sioux was a name given by the Chippewa meaning enemy or snake. In the east, the Sioux had three tribal divisions based on kinship, dialect, and geography. One was originally called Isanyeti, meaning Knife Makers. Today they are known as the Santees and are comprised of four bands: Mdewakanton (Spirit Lake Dwellers), Wahpkute (Shooter among Leaves), Wahpeton (Dwellers among the Leaves), and Sisseton (Fish Scales in the Village). They speak Dakota and have been known as powerful healers and spiritual advocates.
>
> The middle division consisted of the Yanktons and Yanktonnais (Village at the End) who speak a Nakota dialect and are the acknowledged Keepers of the Sacred Pipestone located in western Minnesota.
>
> On the western border are the Tetons (Dwellers on the Prairies). They are the largest band and speak the Lakota dialect. The Tetons moved westward to the plains and west of the Missouri, spreading out and settling in the sacred lands of Paha Sapa, the Black Hills.
>
> As to the Sicangu people, they were moved five times. The Sicangu Lakota (Rosebud Sioux) has sovereignty, so as a nation they have the right to elect their own officials, regulate their own territory, manage tribal affairs, and create and enforce their own tribal laws.

Participants in a talking circle introduced themselves by their relationship to the major bands and tribes. This process established each person's legitimacy and place in society. Many tribal members can recite their genealogy going back several generations. In recalling the history of their people, participants moved from this general introduction to stories of intergenerational trauma, loss, illness, and sorrow. Their comments illustrate the pain these tribes have experienced in being moved to a new location; the illnesses they have suffered, including diabetes; and the progression of fatalism, the need for empowerment, and efforts toward transformation.

Stories of Displacement and Relocation

There were two types of displacement in the tribes' history that affected dietary habits and caused psychosocial problems. Forced relocations from the woodlands of Minnesota to the arid "badlands" of South Dakota in the nineteenth century changed eating habits forever. And forced removal of children from their homes to federal boarding schools disrupted family life, breaking cultural and identity bonds.

Several talking circle participants told stories about ancestors who made the long journey from the Minnesota and Canadian woodlands: "We were moved here from Minnesota. We were forced to relocate here. These are not our lands—we lost them." Tribal identity is intimately bound up with land, and the loss of land was a painful experience. Recounting the tribe's journey to its current reservation site, families recalled the hardships endured, the hunger shared, and the loss of traditions connected to the woodlands lifestyle—traumatic memories handed down through the generations. One participant recalled stories of the move to South Dakota:

> All the things, the little bits of history that I've read, really begin to make sense. Even now we do a lot of things and base it on tradition and how they [the tribes] were treated. Throughout the different moves, the one in South Dakota comes to mind when they talked about the meat or the rations that we were suppose to [be] given. They were spoiled or we didn't even get them. . . . The vats would have about five to six inches of fat in them. And it would smell so bad that no one would want to go near it, to clean it. I mean having to survive on those kinds of rations and things—it's a matter of survival.

As a result of the move, a hunting-gathering lifestyle changed to a sedentary lifestyle. With meat and fish no longer readily available, tribal members came to rely on federal surplus commodities, mainly packaged, high-carbohydrate foods such as flour, sugar, and cereal. "Honest opinion, I think the white people [brought us diabetes]. Like commodities—they don't help."

In the first half of the twentieth century, American Indian children were removed from their homes and placed in distant boarding schools. These forced removals were a lightly veiled attempt to assimilate Indians and disrupt the social structure of the tribes. Boarding school children were forced to wear Western clothing and cut their hair, and they were punished for speaking their Native languages. Entirely new identities were forged as children were given Western names to replace their Indian names. Geographic distance and loss of a shared language eroded the ties between boarding school children and their parents and other relatives. As a result, stated one elder, "our generations face problems of parenthood and cultural identity. Parents and grandparents [of current generations] were taken away to boarding schools, losing language, the guidance of family, and the closeness of culture."

Displacement and relocation play a role in the history of many tribal groups. The federal government carried out numerous policies and experiments, many of them punitive, aimed at changing American Indian culture and assimilating Indians into the larger society. Over the years, these practices traumatized families, resulting in loss of cultural identity and reduced perceptions of self-worth. The damage to emotional health went hand in hand with damage to the physical health of Native peoples.

Stories of Health and Illness

Many talking circle participants pointed out that the etiology of diabetes was not well understood in the community.

> The other thing that I've experienced [is that] the Native American Church [has] done various healings, cancer and those types of things. Diabetes is one of them that they talk about and [question] how does it happen?

> I think living a stressful life [causes diabetes]. I kept worrying about my mom being diabetic. It took her life. I really don't know how a person gets it.

> Some of the elderly, they don't really understand. They don't really understand the cause [of diabetes].

Nonetheless, there was a general awareness of the link between diabetes and eating habits, and some stories associated the disease with changing diets.

> I was like twelve years old when I was giving shots to my grandmother 'cause she had diabetes. I did not understand; she just said you do it like this and so I would give her a shot. After that, that got me curious to find out what it was. It was a physical part of you. This is a disease that has come to us as Native Americans because of the way that our diet has changed in the years since. There are not more buffalo to be eaten. So then we replace it with other things and that is why our bodies are not used to these things.

Losing bodily parts and functions—limbs and eyesight—was described as frightening and disabling, and the specter of early death was always present. Although many remarked that their loved ones never talked about the disease, all knew the inevitable outcome.

They don't know how devastating of a disease it is until they see the real late effects, like someone having to get a foot cut off.

My mom, she never really talked about it. So it was kind of scary when she lost her eyesight and she lost her kidneys.

Then when I ended up diabetic I just couldn't handle it. My father is diabetic too, and they had to amputate his leg. So watching him having a hard time and struggling to move around—to just get off the wheelchair and get on the bed, it just really made me think a lot about this sickness.

What we're talking about around this table is those things that really devastate us. Those things that we seen when our relatives lose their sight or lose limbs.

Participants expressed concern about the impact of diabetes on the future of the Indian people.

I think [a diagnosis of diabetes] scares people. Like with me, because my father died of diabetes complications. I know that, and I think a lot of our people my age, younger, and older all know that diabetes is a problem for our Native people.

Diabetes, or the sugar illness . . . that's such a scary word to us as Native people. It is scary especially when you have had family members that have been called home early [died], because you now have diabetes.

Diabetes [is] like poison due to your body. It affects your whole body. It's killing our people.

Fatalistic beliefs about the inability to prevent, treat, or cure various types of chronic illness were widespread among the participants.

When our Indian people had tuberculosis, there was a lot of them like that, and that was like a wake-up call. When it came, kind of older people had it. It's just something that we have to live with.

This fatalism was particularly marked with respect to diabetes. Talking circle members believed that they would eventually receive a diagnosis of diabetes, that there was nothing that they could do to prevent it, and that there was little or no way to cure the disease.

I was told very young that I would probably get diabetes.

We haven't found out how exactly to do it [prevent diabetes].

I think that it's inevitable. We also learn to live with it.

My grandma and grandpa and my brother and even my sis is diabetic too right now. They control it with diet and with prayers. They really depend on God to help them.

Striving for Empowerment and Transformation

The overall aim of the project was to help participants shed their fatalism about diabetes and reach a state of empowerment, gaining the ability to take charge of their health and make healthy decisions about diet and lifestyle changes. The results of our study showed significant improvement in the form of increased knowledge about diabetes and changes in attitudes toward health. The dialogues showed a progression toward taking control of problems and resolving them, either by finding simple solutions or by learning more about the specific problem. One young mother related her family's efforts to get more exercise:

I like to walk but I'm scared of drunk drivers. I'm scared of dogs too. I told my kids, gee, we should start walking too. So we did. We started going a little ways and turn around and go back. The more we walked the further we got. But it's hard to walk on the road. One evening we were walking and we ran into a rattlesnake. It was dark. I thought I heard something so I looked around and it was a rattlesnake. It was ready to strike. After that we didn't walk on the road. We need some place where we can walk, because there are a lot of drunk drivers on that road too. But I have seen a lot of older people walking. So I think walking is good. We should form groups that would walk together. We can be an example to our own children.

The transformation takes place when participants realize that they have a choice and can take charge of their lives. But this can only happen if they accept the diagnosis of diabetes and take steps to manage it and control its harmful effects.

Then I realized it [diabetes] was with me for life. There's nothing I can do [to] change it. I just got to start taking care of myself, and understand it more.

[Healthy] is being able to do what you want to do. Healthy spiritually, healthy mentally, with that ability to accept learning is a lifelong process.

The stories of the Lakota, Nakota, and Dakota reach back in history and stretch across the Great Plains of North America. The tribes have relied upon storytelling to transmit the history of their people, instruct their young in the ways of their culture, and maintain a dialogue about current issues facing Indian society. In our research study, storytelling revealed the attitudes and beliefs of a people facing illness and trauma due to type 2 diabetes. The "sugar illness" was seen as something introduced by the white man, as a disease that traditional medicine cannot control. It has stolen the futures of tribal members, who first suffer dimming eyesight, then the loss of toes and limbs, and finally early death.

The stories of health and illness told by these tribal communities helped the research team understand the impact of diabetes on a group that saw no possibility of preventing or curing the disease. The intervention and toolkit that were designed relied on these stories to encourage group members to see the fatalism in their attitudes, understand the causes of diabetes, and take steps to control their disease through monitoring and medication. Study results showed a significant improvement in levels of knowledge and a statistically significant decrease in fatalistic beliefs about the ability to prevent and control diabetes. Participants also reported changes in behavior related to eating habits, weight loss, and medication compliance. Oral histories played a crucial role in a process that is gradually helping to change stories of the "sugar illness" from stories of tragedy to stories of healing.

Notes

1. K. J. Acton, N. R. Burrows, K. Moore, L. Querec, L. S. Geiss, and M. M. Engelgau, "Trends in Diabetes Prevalence Among American Indian and Alaska Native Children, Adolescents, and Young Adults," *American Journal of Public Health* 92, no. 9 (2002): 1485–90.

2. F. Hodge, "A Report of a Five-Year Research Study of Diabetes and American Indians on the Winnebago, Pine Ridge, Rosebud, and Yankton Sioux Reservations" (Center for American Indian Research and Education, University of Minnesota, Minneapolis, 2003).

3. R. Tooze, *Storytelling* (Englewood Cliffs, NJ: Prentice Hall, 1959).

4. F. Hodge, L. Fredericks, and B. Rodriguez, "American Indian Women's Talking Circle: A Cervical Cancer Screening and Prevention Project," *Cancer Supplement* 78 (1996): 1592–97.

"*See* What I'm Saying?"
Adding the Visual to Oral History

Karen L. Ishizuka and Robert A. Nakamura

Chris Iijima was so sick that we thought the video life story interview with him might last a half hour if we were lucky. But it was now going into its third hour. A month earlier, when his up-and-down battle with a rare disease called amyloidosis was at a particularly low point, we decided to drop everything and fly to Honolulu from Los Angeles on the chance that he might be able to withstand a short interview. And now he was going on so long the sun was setting and we were losing our light.

Although he had been a law professor at the University of Hawaii for the past seven years, Chris, along with singing his partner Nobuko Miyamoto, was once the foremost troubadour of the Asian American movement of the early 1970s. It was an exhilarating time, when the concept of "Asian American" was generated in opposition to the exotified "Oriental" and in solidarity with other people of color. The term *Asian American* then signified a progressive political stance of self-determination and empowerment, a third world consciousness, that belies the apolitical, demographic designation it has become today. Chris put our issues and newfound identity into song and in so doing gave us something to sing about. An adept performer, honed even sharper by his training as a teacher and attorney, he used his entire body to punctuate his words and drive home his points. When he sang he closed his eyes, tilted his head, and sang as much with his husky frame as with his baritone voice.

> We are the children of the migrant worker.
> We are the children of the concentration camp.
> Sons and daughters of the railroad worker,
> Who will leave their stamp on America.

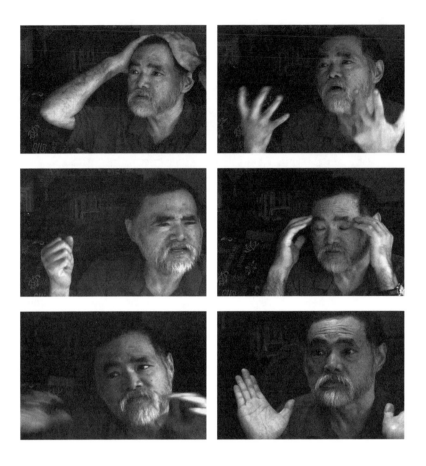

On the afternoon of the life history interview on May 18, 2005, Chris had just returned from the hospital and was tethered to an IV pole, yet he gesticulated emphatically as he spoke. The inflection and modulation in his still-strong voice were accompanied by the coordinated movement of his characteristic wooly eyebrows and uncharacteristically thin arms, the narrowing of his still-vibrant eyes, and expressive shrugs of his now scrawny shoulders.

The interview was informative and insightful, his words well chosen. His zeal for life comes across in the written transcript, and being able to hear the cadence and rhythm of his voice on audiotape adds a sensory element that imbues his words with emotion. But it is the sheer physicality of his delivery caught on videotape that makes his life story interview so spellbinding.

Adding the Visual to the Oral

While not every life story needs to be captured on videotape, this one did. Of course, we didn't know that in advance. We weren't even sure whether Chris's ailing body would tolerate an interview—anyone who's been the subject of a life review knows how exhausting an oral history interview can be. But you never know how good or important a particular interview may turn out to be, what magic moments you might be privy to, or whether this might be the last opportunity to record the person's thoughts and experiences, their visage, their life. Chris died a few months after the interview. While he lives on in the hearts of those who knew him, the intervention of video brings him face to face with those who did not.

Anthropologists, historians, sociologists, and many others use the unstructured, open-ended interview as a method of gaining data about lived experiences. In different periods and within different disciplines, the basic methodology has been called by various names and theorized in a multiplicity of ways. Historians pioneered the term *oral history* in the 1940s as a way of developing historical documentation by interviewing living survivors of the era under investigation.[1] Anthropologists have theorized the methodology as "life history," "person-centered interviewing," and "personal narrative."[2] Some sociologists use the term *life stories* to differentiate topic-directed, focused personal narratives from more comprehensive biographic histories of a person's entire life.[3]

While there are theoretical and methodological differences between terminologies and disciplines, the act and event of the in-depth unstructured interview is common to all. Regardless of label, the interview is a qualitative event that seeks to document the complexity and richness of the lived experience within the intersecting social, cultural, political, and historical dimensions of a person's life. Life stories have the capacity to mediate histories and memories, the personal and the political, hegemony and resistance, the past and the present. This is especially true of interviews that make use of digital video technology. Its ability to capture sight as well as sound, emotion as well as intellect, and background as well as foreground results in visual oral narratives that add layered, nuanced, and compelling testimony to the historical record.

In the 2006 edition of their international anthology on the theory, method, and use of oral history, Robert Perks and Alistair Thomson state, "The advent of video recording was expected to have a major impact on oral history but in actual fact the vast majority of oral history practitioners continue to use audio only."[4] The authors go on to indicate two factors that warrant some discussion here.

First, Perks and Thomson point out that relatively little has been written on the use of video in oral history. The scanty literature they reference dates back in some cases twenty-five years, when video technology was far more unwieldy and obtrusive than it is now.[5] These few texts also focus more on the pragmatics of how to conduct videohistory (based on the technology of the times) than on the impact and effect of its intervention.

Second, they state, "There have been some fears expressed about the impact of the camera and additional crew members on the intimacy of the interview."[6] This is a legitimate concern that should be heeded and respected. Without disregarding the importance of minimizing intrusion, however, it should be noted that cinematic technology has changed significantly. Filming was far more intrusive twenty or thirty years ago, when the bulky 16 mm film camera required a substantial crew, than it is today in the age of digital video and sound. Shooting film requires manipulating the lighting, necessitating the skills of a lighting specialist. Sound recording is not built into the film camera and requires an external microphone, often suspended by a boom pole manned by a sound person and connected to an external tape recorder operated by a second sound person. In contrast, digital video cameras can shoot in low light and have built-in sound recording, eliminating the need for extraneous equipment and crew. They also have a small LCD screen that allows the videographer to compose and shoot without having to physically keep an eye to the viewfinder. This draws less attention to the videographer, and it allows a single person to simultaneously shoot and conduct the interview if necessary. Another factor that mitigates the invasive nature of video interviewing is a sociocultural one. Video cameras have become customary objects of everyday life in our society. Many broadcast-quality camcorders look very similar to those that the narrator and his or her friends and family might use themselves. In fact, small camcorders have become almost as commonplace as point-and-shoot still cameras and may be more familiar and hence less intimidating than the audio tape recorder, which is far less used by the general public.

At the risk of stating the obvious, the primary difference between video life history and traditional oral history is the addition of the visual element. By this we mean that the goals of video recording are not fundamentally different from those of oral recording, but video builds upon the oral by adding visual evidence. In other words, what is documented is not just the content of the words or the sound of the voice but also the narrator's expressions, gestures, and body language. People are not audio-only communicators. Some people talk with their hands or even with their entire bodies. Their shoulders rise with emotion or shrug in disgust. They clasp their hands in joy or smack their forehead for emphasis. Even those who don't talk with their hands use their eyes and move their heads, however subtly. One cannot speak without also moving some part of the body. The raise of an eyebrow can add irony to an otherwise straightforward statement. The widening of the eyes denotes wonder or surprise. A smirk conveys contempt, a grin delight. A frown expresses displeasure or maybe intense concentration. The body communicates desire, emotions, feelings. It speaks a language that can only be expressed physically and hence must be recorded visually. Young people on the street know this, as is evident in their slang. "You *feel* me?" and "*See* what I'm saying?" connote the visceral communication not conveyed in the more cognitive "Do you understand what I mean?"

The capability of video to capture nonverbal communication and surroundings, however, does not necessarily make video life history better. There are occasions when videotaping would not be appropriate, just as there are instances when oral tape recording or even note taking are not appropriate either. Our predilection for video does not negate our respect for and appreciation of text and the aural. As an anthropologist schooled initially in the concept of life history, Karen feels that published texts have the authority to put people of color into the canon of American history and culture, an agency that video does not have. Unlike audio and video documents, books and articles have the capacity to be reread, highlighted, footnoted, and cited. On the other hand, Bob's background in photojournalism convinced him that life stories can be told solely with pictures, eliding or minimizing words altogether. And we are both fans of radio documentaries and spoken word. At this point we have a substantial body of work as community-based documentary filmmakers who have used personal narratives to make films on the Japanese American experience. This essay summarizes our approach to conducting video life histories to document, preserve, and present Asian American histories and experiences in the hope that it might be useful for other cultural workers of color.

The Agency of Video Life History

Film and video have long been used in the field of anthropology, spawning subdisciplines such as ethnographic film and visual anthropology. In 1975 visual anthropologist Colin Young wrote, "The faith that many social scientists have in film as providing them with 'an objective recording instrument' is touching and almost sentimental."[7] Are social scientists more sophisticated now? Yes and no. We may be more visually literate, but we should be mindful that we are also products of a society that is increasingly shaped and created by mass communications media. As media has become more global and omnipresent, social scientists as well as the general public are at once hip to visual effects and manipulation and at the same time accustomed to and dependent upon mass media for information. We learn about the world not so much through direct experience as through television and movies, newspapers and magazines, and the Internet. As media-savvy as we think we are, we cannot help but unconsciously accept and act upon media content even as we challenge its veracity intellectually. Therefore, those of us who use media as a tool would be wise to be attentive and aware of how it works and what impact it has.

To begin to understand the agency of the visual life history, one must first understand the authority of the life history itself. Regardless of its utility in gathering data, the life story interview constitutes a specific type of communicative event that is situated within a particular social context. Whether videotaped or not, the interview is a privileged temporal space that lies outside the parameters of everyday life. It is partly dialogue, but it is not bounded by such rules of social conversation as turn taking and jointly produced discourse, since the center of attention is on one participant and not the other. It is partly a monologue but one that is marked by spontaneity rather than rehearsal. By participating in a life story interview, both interviewer and interviewee implicitly agree to abide by certain norms. The social position that each normally occupies outside of the synthesized situation is moved to the background and the encounter is structured to conform to the roles of interviewer and interviewee. Both have prescribed functions and expected standards of behavior and interaction.

For the interviewees or narrators, the life story interview is an occasion in which they are asked to tell about their life and experiences without being judged. It is a constructed event in which the narrator can be, and indeed is expected to be, honest and forthcoming. And what is said is to be taken at face value, without moral judgment. There are no right or wrong responses. Therefore, the life history interview needs to take place in a safe space within which personal opinions and thoughts are offered freely and received uncontested and unevaluated. While dates and facts are checked for historical accuracy, it is the narrator's subjective experience of the event that is the raison d'être of the life history interview.

Although the narrator is the center of attention, the interviewer is in charge. It is up to him or her to set the stage and create that safe space in which genuine memories, thoughts, opinions, and feelings are free to emerge. While the interviewee is expected to be spontaneous and unrehearsed, the researcher should be prepared with a toolbox of questions and promptings to bring out the most and the best in the interviewee. The researcher has ultimate responsibility for the success of the interview. In academic parlance, success is defined by the efficacy and utility of the data. In a community-based context, we as researchers define a successful encounter as one that is as meaningful to the interviewee as it is to us. In either case, the interview dyad is an unequal relationship, with the interviewer in the driver's seat.

When the life story is videotaped, another layer of intervention is imposed that influences the hermeneutic nature of the event in a variety of subtle ways. There is agency to the act of videotaping that exceeds the capture of sight and sound. It not only hears and sees, it does. The act of videotaping is not transparent, without effect. It is not the technological equivalent of the fly on the wall or the all-seeing eye. What does videotaping do in a life history besides capture sight and sound? Does it alter or affect the quality of the experience and the data? If so, how? This topic requires far more detailed discussion than is possible here, but we would like to briefly point out two related aspects of its agency: it alters the social construction of data collection, and it assumes an audience, which functions to enhance the performativity of the interview.

The video interview is conducted, enacted, and performed within a field of action. Thus the focal event of the video interview cannot be examined outside the context in which it takes place. On the surface, the context of the interview consists of the setting and its participants. But each is problematized in dynamic and interactive ways. Most obviously, the video life story interview adds a third participant, the videographer, to the conventional oral history duo of interviewee and interviewer. The videographer alters the event by his or her added presence and also complicates it by not being ratified in the act of interviewing, only in its recording. She or he is a silent partner who occupies a liminal space in the traditional pairing of interviewer and interviewee. The videographer's job is to see and hear—but only from a distance, through the veil and mechanism of the video camera.

Yet the videographer is not an inanimate picture taker, but rather a living, breathing presence who increases the audience of the event. The interviewer, as the person to whom the interviewee speaks, constitutes the primary if informal audience. The videographer, although not addressed and not the intended hearer, is nonetheless privy to the life story and hence creates an audience of two. In addition, regardless of those in attendance, the very act of recording the interview on videotape presumes yet another audience—an imagined one. In a video life history the narrator is speaking for the record. His or her visage and words are being documented to be seen and heard by someone at some later date—for posterity, so to speak. Even if the interview ends up being archived without being transcribed, heard, or seen, the act of videotaping presumes an audience. And an audience is constitutive of performance. Indeed, a good life history interview is a performance with the narrator as actor and the researcher as director. This is not to be taken in a dramaturgical sense. Yet to the extent that the interviewee enacts what is asked of him or her—that is, to tell the story of his or her life with honesty and substance—the interview constitutes verbal art.

The medium of the moving image also adds a performative quality. It has the power to represent or misrepresent. When used effectively, it can be either enlightening and hence beneficial or misleading and thereby dangerous. If the art of oral history begs the question of authority as well as agency, the visual life history does so even more. Those of us who use the camera as a means of data collection would be wise to turn a critical eye on ourselves and provide a reflexive account of how we do what we do, resulting in a more transparent and rigorous analysis of videotaping as a methodology.

EthnoCommunications

Conceptually, a guiding principle of our work is the centrality of community. By community we mean ethnically based populations determined not by geography or even strictly by race as much as by heritage, common experience, and self-identity. When we say we are community-based, we mean that we share the heritage, experience, and identity that we depict. By joining other Asian American, Chicana/o, African American, and

Native American cultural workers who approach community-centered practices as political acts, we fulfill the cultural roles of seekers and guardians of memories, tellers and recorders of stories, keepers and makers of history, and griots of consciousness.

We practice an approach to community film we call "EthnoCommunications," which responds to the need for ethnic communities to gain sovereignty over their own representations and make their own voices heard. EthnoCommunications is a form of counterhegemonic film practice whose goal is to document, preserve, and present marginalized communities from a community perspective. Its central principle is that such filmmaking is done by and for the communities in question rather than by and for outside producers or audiences.

This inside-out (versus outside-in) dynamic is key to rediscovering and reclaiming lost or endangered histories, listening to collective memories to find submerged personal meanings, and sharing the burden of representation. Anthropologist Eric Wolf wrote an influential book titled *Europe and the People without History* (1982).[8] It builds on the dichotomy between "the West" and "the Rest," but Wolf goes further by specifying Europe as constituting the West and classifying the rest (of us), being non-European, as people without history. Without a history, we have no shoulders upon which to stand. Unless we can find, remember, write, and tell our own histories, they are in danger of being lost. The theory and practice of EthnoCommunications was conceived to enable ethnic communities in the United States to document and preserve their own histories and cultures and in the process reclaim their past, redefine their present, and reenvision their future. It proposes that theory and practice can be integrated in meaningful ways through collaborative projects with people and institutions in and outside the academy. As practitioners of EthnoCommunications, we believe that people have the capability and authority to interpret their own histories and cultures through their own eyes.

The concept of EthnoCommunications originated in a short-lived program of the same name developed to recruit people of color into the film department at the University of California, Los Angeles, in the early 1970s. Bob was part of that program, lured from working for the renowned design team of Charles and Ray Eames and a successful career in commercial photography and photojournalism. Yearning to apply his professional skills to telling his community's stories, he joined fellow graduate students Luis Ruiz, Sylvia Morales, Larry Clark, Moctezuma Esparza, and others in a commitment to make the program their own. They eschewed the top-down, outside-in tradition of ethnographic filmmaking in favor of developing a bottom-up, inside-out, community-based film practice. And they went on to become pioneering filmmakers in their communities.

From a theoretical perspective, EthnoCommunications is rooted in the concept of "third cinema," which was first articulated by Latin American filmmakers in 1969. The term *third cinema* was coined by Argentine filmmakers Fernando Solanas and Octavio Getino in their seminal article, "Hacia un Tercer Cine" (Toward a Third Cinema). They defined third cinema—not to be confused with third *world* cinema—as a postcolonial cinema of resistance, arising from a determination of community-based filmmakers to be agents of their own history. Third cinema is formulated in contradistinction to both "first cinema," the mainstream, capitalistic film industry epitomized by Hollywood, and "second cinema," individualistic avant-garde art film associated with European cinematic auteurs. Later, Cuban filmmaker Julio García Espinosa published "For an Imperfect Cinema," which, according to Paul Willemen, argued for "an end to the division between art and life and therefore between professional intellectuals such as filmmakers and critics and 'the people.'"[9] In the 1980s Teshome Gabriel further theorized third cinema as a guardian of popular memory committed to a liberative, decolonizing vision. His articulation of filmmakers occupying "the same cultural and historic ambience as people depicted on the screen" was particularly cogent for the development of EthnoCommunications theory. Gabriel added that third cinema filmmakers' "history and emotional milieu conditions them to focus on those with whom they are inextricably linked."[10]

Bob founded the Center for EthnoCommunications in 1996 within the UCLA Asian American Studies Center. Its purpose is to create meaningful linkages between the university and diverse ethnic communities in Los Angeles through collaborative projects using digital media and communications technologies. EthnoCommunications seeks to expose students to social change and community-based media issues, methodologies, and strategies and to create opportunities for students to combine university learning with emerging media skills in direct community service. To this end, an EthnoCommunications curriculum was developed to teach community media theory and digital video production to nonfilm majors over three quarters. Originally designed for undergraduates, the program soon attracted graduate students who wanted to incorporate community-based media research and methodology and digital video production into their thesis projects. In 2002 the Center for EthnoCommunications entered into a partnership with the Little Tokyo Service Center (LTSC) in downtown Los Angeles to establish the Downtown Community Media Center, furthering the goal of creating media service and learning opportunities in local communities of color. Through this collaboration, UCLA EthnoCommunications students have worked through LTSC to conduct video life histories with residents of LTSC's low-cost housing project and document a variety of community events.

The EthnoCommunications approach calls for a heightened sense of reflexivity and sensitivity on the part of community-based filmmakers and scholars like us. As members of the communities we seek to understand and portray, we are insiders. As Gabriel indicated, we occupy the same cultural and historic context as people depicted on the screen or the page. Yet we recognize that by virtue of that seeking, whether as filmmakers or as scholars, we are necessarily looking in from the outside. This dual vantage point demands that when working with our respective communities, we are diligent in speaking *from* our communities rather than *for* them.

When the two of us work together, we try to make the videotaping of life stories as simple and unobtrusive as possible. This means working with available light, which eliminates the need for external lighting equipment. We use radio lavalier microphones that operate remotely and remain out of sight and hopefully out of mind once clipped to the narrator's shirt. And we compose a minimal crew, usually consisting of Karen as interviewer and Bob as videographer. For longer interview sessions, or if we think gender would make a difference in putting the narrator at ease, both of us might conduct the interview; in these cases we engage a videographer, usually our son Tadashi Nakamura, with whom we work as a filmmaking team. In other cases, for example when interviewing young people who might be inhibited from talking freely in front of older adults, Tad has acted as both interviewer and videographer. He has been surprisingly successful at this: both roles require concentration and focus, making it difficult for one person to do them simultaneously, but he has achieved ease and self-disclosure on the part of the narrators along with high-quality technical recording of sight and sound.

We have undertaken three basic types of projects in which life histories play a dominant role. The first are community-based documentary films that have screened on public television and at film festivals around the world, as well as in community centers, classrooms, and living rooms across the nation. The second are memorial video life histories that have been screened at funerals and commemorative tributes. The third category consists of video life history projects as documentation. These extensive video interviews, like traditional oral history projects, are organized around specific topics or historical periods.

Documentary Films Based on Life Stories

Manzanar (1971), Bob's first film, is a lyrical, introspective account of his boyhood years in a World War II concentration camp for Japanese Americans.[11] It was the first film on the camps from an inmate's perspective and was made at a time when the history of the camps was still little known. The U.S. government understandably did not publicize this history, and the schools didn't teach it. The community of former inmates had been silenced from within by the humiliation of having been betrayed by one's own government and from without by the official line that the mass incarceration was a military necessary for national security.

The camera takes a first-person point of view, sometimes meandering, sometimes running frantically through the ruins at the abandoned site of Manzanar, the camp where Bob was detained for three years as a child. Dissatisfied with a written narration, and having suppressed what little he could remember, Bob decided to take on the role of interviewer and probe his own subconscious memories by asking himself questions about his early years in camp. Equipped with a reel-to-reel Nagra sound recorder, Bob began the self-interview late one night. Continuing into the early morning, he discovered that as he grew more and more tired he dropped his guard and his usual inhibitions about talking about camp loosened, allowing long-forgotten memories to surface. He edited the hours-long tape-recorded interview into an intimate voice-over for the film. Transcribed, the narration is only three paragraphs, a little over 1,500 words. Judiciously spaced over the twenty-minute film, the words augment the visuals in the telling of the story, like a photo essay.

> I was only six years old, so I really can't remember anything definite. It's just vague impressions. . . . One incident [that] kind of sticks in my mind was when the FBI came and took away our next-door neighbor. He was very active in judo and kendo, and I used to play with his two daughters. As a matter of fact, I was at their home when the two FBI agents came. I remember looking at them through the screen door and then later my neighbor's wife telling me to go home. I remember that evening my dad was very, very agitated because he was also very active in judo.

Wataridori: Birds of Passage (1975) tells the history of Japanese in the United States through the life stories of three Issei, immigrants from Japan.[12] Bob conducted preliminary interviews with over a hundred Issei. From these, he selected twenty for more in-depth interviews before deciding on three principals—one woman and two men—whose stories reflected a range of immigrant experiences. Bob wanted engaging life stories, but he did not want to sacrifice the core historical experience in favor of fascinating accounts that that would be out of the ordinary. He chose a widow because widowhood was common among Issei women, a reflection of the longevity of females compared to males and also of the fact that Issei wives were usually much younger than their husbands due to immigration laws. He selected two men who immigrated for different reasons—one for financial gain and the other for pure adventure.

All three narrators had originally intended to return to Japan, hence the use of *wataridori*, which means "birds of passage," in the film's title. Their accounts covered their childhoods in Japan, their immigration to the United States in the 1920s, and their experiences of raising families and growing old in their adopted country. The voice-over narration was edited from the written transcripts. Because the narrators were Japanese-speaking, English-speaking actors read their words.

> Life was always hard in Kagoshima. Even as a young boy, I always heard, "Go to America! Go to America, where money is scattered like winter leaves."
>
> I have been a gardener since the day after I arrived in Los Angeles. As I look back, I don't know how I did it. Riding a bicycle with a lawn-mower tied on the back, edger strapped to the front and a rake in one hand! Very often little boys would throw stones and chant "Jap! Jap!" as I rode down the street.
>
> My wife and I used to talk about returning to Japan. But in my mind that is no longer possible. My place is here, in this country, with my grandchildren and the grandchildren of my old comrades. The Japan I left fifty years ago no longer exists.

Looking Like the Enemy (1995) is a video essay consisting of testimonials by nineteen American soldiers of Asian descent who spoke, most for the first time, about the harrowing experiences they faced in wars against Asians—World War II, the Korean War, and the Vietnam War.[13] Spanning generations and wars, this film was structured solely around their video life stories, with very little documentary content other than shadowy newsreel footage of each war to set the stage and provide a brief historical context.

The men told of racism in the military and of disturbingly close calls in which they were mistaken for the enemy. They also shared personal nightmares and the horrors of combat that soldiers rarely discuss. During some of the interviews, the veteran's wife sat listening from another room. Inevitably she would tell us that it was the first time she had heard her husband talk about the war. While the focus of the film was on the veterans' words, and we used what are often disparagingly called "talking heads," one reviewer commented, "The soldiers' faces, as they share their experiences, make history come alive."[14]

During World War II, all of the armed forces in the United States—Army, Navy, Marine Corps, Air Force—were segregated. One narrator said, "We were fighting two wars. One for American democracy. The other against the prejudice toward us in America." By the time of the Korean conflict, the units were integrated, but American soldiers of Asian descent were still mistaken for the enemy. "And when I got hit, I said "Hey!" But they [U.S. soldiers] would just look at me. They thought I was Korean, and they'd just go right by." Several Asian American Vietnam vets recounted being singled out in training and pointed to as an example of what the enemy looks like. One recalled, "I was placed on a podium one day . . . and I was called a gook. 'This is what the enemy looks like! Kill it before it kills you!'"

All the interviews for this film were conducted by the two of us: Bob on camera and Karen interviewing. This minimal crew lent an intimacy to the setting despite the presence of the camera. As a veteran himself, Bob felt a kinship with our narrators although he had never experienced combat. We were concerned that Karen, as a female interviewer, might not be well suited to the "macho" yet emotionally delicate topic of war. However, that did not seem to be an inhibiting factor, as the level of self-disclosure the men engaged in was courageously deep. Our hunch is that they responded genuinely because we convinced them both of our sincere interest in their stories and of the need to pass their experiences on to others, especially to young people. To this end we took considerable time to talk with them beforehand regarding the purpose and intent of the project. In many cases, we had a trusted friend or family member of the veteran introduce us and/or set up the interview.

A Song for Ourselves (2009) is a documentary based on the charismatic life history interview we conducted with Chris Iijima.[15] The documentary began as a memorial video that was screened at services for Chris across the country (discussed further in the next section). While built around the life history interview, the film also included heart-rending interviews with Chris's widow, two teenage sons, parents, singing partner, and best friend. A *Song for Ourselves* is both a highly personal look at the artistic and cultural legacy of the early Asian American movement, told through Chris's life and music, and the story of how his loved ones are coping with his death.

In the interviews with Chris's sons, ages thirteen and sixteen, our son Tadashi, who directed the film, also acted as both interviewer and videographer. We were well aware that the two young teenagers might find it difficult to talk about their dad's death on videotape, and we worked to create an environment in which they would feel safe and comfortable. We knew that neither of us, as older people, would be the interviewer of choice in this case. In addition, Chris's younger son was initially not sure he wanted to be interviewed or be part of the film. He eventually agreed, perhaps reassured—or compelled—by his older brother's participation. Although Karen usually sets up and coordinates the interviews, we left all the logistics up to Tad and the boys. As these excerpts attest, both boys were wonderfully open and forthcoming, showing that video life histories of technical and substantive quality can be conducted by one person without assistance.

> SIXTEEN-YEAR-OLD ALAN: I just really hate it whenever someone brought up Dad. Like how he was a great guy and how, you know, he had a great life, all that bullshit. Like he did but I want him here now. It doesn't matter how great a life he had, I want him here now. He's my dad, he should be here. I mean, shit's not gonna be okay, it's just not.

> THIRTEEN-YEAR-OLD CHRISTOPHER: I turned to Dad and said, "Dad, what happens if you die and there's no heaven or hell, it's just oblivion?" And Dad just turned to me and said, "When I was your age I also thought about that and then I decided, 'Who cares? Who really cares? I mean, what happens in death, we're going to figure that out when we go because no one can tell. We'll just figure that out.'"

Life History Memorial Videos

One of the most unusual and noteworthy ways we have melded life history and video is by producing short video profiles for a narrator's funeral or memorial service. Memorial visual presentations in the form of slide shows or PowerPoint presentations are increasingly screened at funerals and especially at nonreligious memorial events. Indeed, there are now commercial ventures that will stitch together family photographs against canned music, just as there are business enterprises that conduct oral or video life histories for profit. To date, we have been asked to create five memorial video profiles based on life history interviews we have conducted. Our son and partner Tadashi Nakamura edits the video life histories into a mini-documentary about the person, incorporating B-roll—supplementary images such as photographs, documents, and live-action footage that illustrate or enhance the narrator's interview. The three of us donate all materials and labor. Memorial videos are an example of another way that video life histories can serve community.

The first memorial video featured an elderly man interviewed as part of the program of the Downtown Community Media Center, the partnership between the UCLA Center for EthnoCommunications and the Little Tokyo Service Center. The purpose of the community project was to document people living in subsidized housing in Little Tokyo, Los Angeles. Eddie was one of the many single men who live alone on the fringes of this commercial area, which was once a thriving ethnic center but has now become gentrified with high-rise condos and artists' lofts. One rainy day he was killed instantly by a car while crossing the street. Eddie had been an avid picture taker at community events and spent a sizable share of his meager income on having prints made for those who appeared in his photos. As part of his life history interview, we also videotaped him walking through Little Tokyo delivering pictures to friends, sometimes slipping the prints beneath closed storefront doors. Showing the video at his small funeral provided a tribute to Eddie's spirit and a history of one of the many little-known members who make up a community.

Three other memorial videos were made for community leaders at the request of their families, who knew we had conducted video interviews of them. To supplement the video life histories, their families provided still photographs that lent visual continuity and interest to the interview.

A fifth memorial video was the tribute to Chris Iijima. It was shown at commemorative events in Los Angeles, New York, and San Francisco, and DVD copies were made available for a donation to the fund set up to help cover his medical expenses. Like the other memorial videos, it centered on a video life history conducted previously. In this case, however, because Chris was a well-known community singer and songwriter, a treasure trove of documentation was unearthed after he died—not only still photographs but also audio and film recordings of performances. Among them were a

1974 appearance on the *Mike Douglas Show*, where he was introduced by John Lennon and Yoko Ono; 16 mm film footage that Bob had shot of Chris's performances in community settings throughout the 1970s; and home movies supplied by Chris's family and friends. The resulting memorial video also helped us to secure grants to produce the documentary *A Song for Ourselves* (2009).

Video Life History Projects

In addition to documentary films and memorial videos, we have carried out video life history projects that, like their oral history counterparts, organize a series of extensive life stories around a central theme.

"Eye to Eye: Asian American Arts and Artists" (2000) is a series of sixteen video life histories of contemporary Asian Pacific American artists. They include poets, painters, writers, musicians, actors, and dancers—some established, some emerging. To supplement the video life histories, we videotaped the artists showing examples of their work in their respective studios and workshops. Still photos of them growing up and photos of their art were gathered and digitized. Together, the video life history, the tour of their creative environment, and the gallery of photos provide a visual archive of the artists and how they work.

These visual elements were compiled on one to three videocassettes per artist. The cassettes were accompanied by a booklet that included the full transcript of the interview keyed by timecode to the videocassette, as well as a résumé of the artist's work. The project was conceptualized and conducted in 1998 and 1999 and produced on analog videotape before digital media technology was fully developed. As digital technology has emerged, the analog module on one artist has been converted into DVD format with its contents chapterized for ease of access and study. This provides a prototype for the possible formats that digital video life histories could take.

"Arts of Activism: The Cultural Legacy of the Early Asian American Movement" is our current video life history project. Its goals are to document, preserve, and make known the cultural legacy of the early Asian American movement (1968–1978) through video life histories of artists and cultural workers who used art and culture as a platform for protest and a tool for social change. Video life history is used as the primary strategy for exploring the role that artistic expression played in reflecting and creating the culture of the Asian American movement of the 1970s.

When the movement began, many of us, never having learned about our histories in school, realized that oral interviews of our immigrant grandparents could provide the insight we were seeking. Despite our grandparents' advanced age and our own linguistic limitations, members of our generation carried out many such oral and life history projects. When we learned about the World War II camps, oral histories with our parents and other former inmates became a primary means of research and education.

Now, leading figures in the early Asian American movement are in their fifties and sixties. Many have already passed away, and several have suffered strokes or other debilitating illnesses; memories are growing dim. It is urgent to document the lives of these now-historic figures before it is too late. Life histories conducted on the generations before them have provided primary data that enabled and encouraged secondary analysis and interpretation in the form of books, films, and other media to be created. Recording the stories and experiences of these Asian American artist-activists will add to the continuum of scholarship and understanding of the American experience.

Conclusion: Seeing in Color

You would not think people of color in this country would be so invisible. Race is visual. We are classified, circumscribed, and characterized by our color, by being nonwhite. Yet, from the actors, models, and newsworthy personalities depicted on television and in newspapers and magazines, at least until the late 1960s, one might think that the United States was all white. Or more accurately, as the late poet Audre Lorde put it, "white, thin, male, young, heterosexual, christian, and financially secure."[16] For decades, people of color rarely saw themselves reflected in popular media. And when we were, it did not show us as we really are. Except for the occasional maid, cook, or gardener, and later the perfunctory sidekick, minion, or other subordinate, we were invisible.

Oral history gives everyday folks a place at the table of History with a capital H. And for people of color, because we have been hidden from view—even from ourselves—it is not only important to record our thoughts and hear our words, it is important to see our faces. One of the purposes of oral history has been to give names to the countless masses who live and make history and voice to those who are not often heard. For people of color, video life history allows us, and others, to see ourselves as we are. This is the special agency that video life histories can have for communities of color.

Epilogue

On that warm Honolulu day in 2005, Chris sat for the interview in his favorite easy chair in the living room of his modest apartment. We were mindful to crop out the ever-present IV stand so the focal point would be Chris rather than his illness. The soothing trade winds of the Manoa Valley cooled the room so we didn't have to control for the rumbling starts and stops of the air conditioner, which, while rarely an issue in normal conversation, seems to roar distractingly on video.

Chris's thick eyebrows danced above his piercing dark eyes, now even more vibrant and penetrating against his sallow, gaunt face. We were concerned about tiring him and often asked if he needed a break—until he put an end to our repeated queries with an emphatic "I'm fine! This is energizing!" Indeed, his vigor was apparent in the enthusiasm with which he spoke, marked by gesturing, changes in tempo, use of exclamations, eye contact, and intense vocalizing. His fortitude and resolve amplified the agency of the interview. As he became more and more animated, his audience grew more and more attentive. His father came in from the kitchen. His two teenage sons came down from their rooms and sat on the steps to listen. His mother came to sit with his wife at the dining room table. This physically sick and frail man had everyone mesmerized, because for the video interview, in front of the camera, like an actor who can transform himself into another person, Chris became more his old self than he had been in almost two years.

Even now, almost five years after his death, to see him in the interview—leaning forward in his chair, clenching his hands and slapping his forehead, raising those wooly eyebrows and peering unabashedly into your eyes—is to bring him into the room with you with the intimacy that oral history seeks to attain. The interview, which was centered around the Asian American movement, was drawing to a close and it was getting almost too dark to shoot when Chris suddenly said, "I know what I want to say. Can I say one more thing?"

> I think what gets lost, all the time, in any of this is . . . in the midst of all of this, it was a tremendous amount of fun! When your life is changing, when your values are changing, when things are alive and vibrating and

popping all over the place, being a part of that is just *fun*! I used to feel bad for people who weren't involved because I felt they were missing out! Part of the reason people were attracted may not have been the politics, may not have been the voice, but it's where it was happening. It was where the party was! . . . You would meet people who were strange and bizarre. You had experiences you would have never had before. It was a *blast!* . . . And I think that's what we never talk about—what a great amount of fun it was!

From video life history of Chris K. Iijima, May 18, 2005, Honolulu, Hawaii. Interviewers: Karen L. Ishizuka and Robert A. Nakamura. Videographer: Tadashi Nakamura.

Notes

1. For more on oral history, see Ronald J. Grele, ed., *Envelopes of Sound: The Art of Oral History* (New York: Praeger, 1991); Michael Frish, *A Shared Authority: Essays on the Craft and Meaning of Oral History and Public History* (Albany: State University of New York Press, 1990); Sherna Berger Gluck and Daphne Patai, eds., *Women's Words: The Feminist Practice of Oral History* (New York: Routledge, 1991); and Thomas L. Charlton, Lois E. Myers, and Rebecca Sharpless, eds., *Handbook of Oral History* (Lanham, MD: AltaMira Press, 2006).

2. On life history, see Lew Langness, *The Life History in Anthropological Science* (New York: Holt, Rinehart and Winston, 1965); Lew Langness and Gelya Frank, *Lives: An Anthropological Approach to Biography* (Novato, CA: Chandler and Sharp, 1981); Lawrence C. Watson and Barbara Watson-Franke, *Interpreting Life Histories: An Anthropological Inquiry* (New Brunswick, NJ: Rutgers University Press, 1985) and Gelya Frank, "Anthropology and Individual Lives: The Story of the Life History and History of the Life Story," *American Anthropologist* 81, no. 1 (1995): 141–48. On person-centered interviewing, see Robert I. Levy and Douglas Hollan, "Person-Centered Interviewing and Observation in Anthropology," in *Handbook of Methods in Cultural Anthropology*, ed. H. R. Bernard (Walnut Creek, CA: AltaMira Press, 1998); and Douglas Hollan, "Setting a New Standard: The Person-Centered Interviewing and Observation of Robert I. Levy," *Ethos* 33, no. 4 (2008): 459–66. On personal narrative, see Elinor Ochs and Lisa Capps, "Narrating the Self," *Annual Review of Anthropology* 25 (1996): 19–43; and Elinor Ochs and

Lisa Capps, *Living Narrative: Creating Lives in Everyday Storytelling* (Cambridge, MA: Harvard University Press, 2001).

3. Daniel Bertaux and Martin Kohli, "The Life Story Approach: A Continental View," *Annual Review of Sociology* 10 (1984): 215–37; Faye Ginsburg, "Procreation Stories: Reproduction, Nurturance, and Procreation in Life Narratives of Abortion Activists," *American Ethnologist* 14, no. 4 (1987): 623–36.

4. Robert Perks and Alistair Thomson, eds., *The Oral History Reader*, 2nd ed. (New York: Routledge, 2006), 119.

5. Brad Jolly, *Videotaping Local History* (Nashville: American Association for State and Local History, 1982); Terri A. Schorzman, *A Practical Introduction to Videohistory: The Smithsonian Institution and Alfred P. Sloan Foundation Experiment* (Malabar, FL: Krieger, 1993); Donald A. Ritchie, "Videotaping Oral History," in *Doing Oral History: A Practical Guide*, 2nd ed. (New York: Oxford University Press, 2003).

6. Perks and Thomson, *Oral History Reader*, 119.

7. Colin Young, "Observational Cinema," in *Principles of Visual Anthropology*, ed. Paul Hockings (The Hague: Mouton, 1975), 100.

8. Eric R. Wolf, *Europe and the People without History* (Berkeley: University of California Press, 1982).

9. Paul Willemen, "The Third Cinema Question: Notes and Reflections," in *Questions of Third Cinema*, ed. Jim Pines and Paul Willemen (London: BFI Publishing, 1989), 5. Julio García Espinosa's "For an Imperfect Cinema" was originally published in *Cine Cubano*, no. 66/67, in 1970.

10. Teshome Gabriel, introduction to "American Black Film Practice: Towards a Conceptual Framework," a retrospective of independent Black American cinema (University of California, Los Angeles, 1984).

11. Robert A. Nakamura, *Manzanar*, 16 mm, 16 minutes (Visual Communications, distributed by the Center for Asian American Media, San Francisco, 1971).

12. Robert A. Nakamura, *Wataridori: Birds of Passage*, 16 mm, 36 minutes, color (Visual Communications, distributed by the Center for Asian American Media, San Francisco, 1975).

13. Robert A. Nakamura and Karen L. Ishizuka, *Looking Like the Enemy*, video, 52 minutes, color (produced and distributed by the Japanese American National Museum, Los Angeles, 1995).

14. Unpublished review by Karen Kushell of DreamWorks, 1995.

15. Tadashi Nakamura, *A Song for Ourselves*, video, 34 minutes, color (Center for EthnoCommunications, distributed by the Center for Asian American Media, San Francisco, 2009).

16. Audre Lorde, "Age, Race, Class, and Sex: Women Redefining Difference," in *Out There: Marginalization and Contemporary Cultures*, ed. Russell Ferguson, Martha Gever, Trinh T. Minh-ha, and Cornel West (New York: New Museum of Contemporary Art; Cambridge, MA: MIT Press, 1990), 281–87.

Not In Their Plans

Gentrification, Latina/os, and the Practice of Community Oral History

Nancy Raquel Mirabal

> As a historian, I have learned that, in fact, not everyone who reaches
> back into history can survive it.
> —Elizabeth Kostova, *The Historian*

> We are not in their plans.
> —Rosario Anaya, Mission District resident and activist, 1999

What does it mean to develop and create a community oral history within
and among populations of color? Do oral history projects ever really
influence and change the communities where they are conducted? Can
oral historical methodologies ever transition into activist scholarship?
Should they?

In 1999 I organized and directed a community oral history project on
gentrification and the resulting displacement of Latina/os from the Mission
District, a longstanding Latina/o neighborhood in San Francisco. It began
as an assignment in my undergraduate Latina/o oral history and theories
course, asking students to investigate why so many Latina/o residents were
being forced out of the Mission. I never expected the project to last more
than a year. But as students and colleagues learned about the project, they
got involved, and it grew. It evolved into an eight-year oral history project
and archive that involved close to eighty students along with an array of
local activists, colleagues, residents, poets, and digital mural artists.

The students in the course named the project "La Misión: Voices
of Resistance." They carried out interviews, set up a website, created an
archive, and collected census data, government documents, poster art,
maps, and other primary sources. They expanded the scope of the project

by working with nonprofits, attending planning commission meetings, and becoming active in the local fight against displacement.

Within a few years, it was clear that the questions that had inspired the project did not fully explore the larger issues surrounding gentrification and redevelopment. These included the uses of a reformulated public discourse to redefine space, the erasure of racialized populations from the public discourse, and the gendered, heteronormative, and masculinist meanings attached to spatial knowledge. What started as an experiment in oral historical methodologies soon turned into a larger discussion about who has the right to dictate the use of urban space—and, moreover, who has the right to tell the story of gentrification and displacement.

This chapter probes the uneasy and imprecise practice of oral historical methods by examining the process used to organize and conduct a community-centered oral history project built upon a multiplicity of experiences and voices. It highlights the emotional and difficult work of doing oral history on a polarizing and painful topic, and it documents how the "La Misión" project forced us to rethink the relationship between oral historical methodologies and working-class communities of color in San Francisco and elsewhere.[1]

We found that the history we were researching extends into the present. Despite the dot-com bust, the collapse of the housing bubble, and the recession, gentrification in San Francisco continues. The fact that a crumbling economy has not halted it challenges the commonly accepted notion that gentrification is solely rooted in market forces. Clearly, there are other factors involved in determining the gentrification of certain neighborhoods and not others. This realization led us to a reassessment of how race, immigration, gender, citizenship, sexuality, and economic class continue to play a role in the gentrification of neighborhoods years after the boom, during one of the most difficult economic downturns in California's recent history.

Gentrification and Racial Displacement in the Mission

In the mid-1990s a number of San Francisco neighborhoods were being gentrified, including the Western Addition, Bayview, Potrero Hill, South of Market, and the Embarcadero. Yet one neighborhood in particular, the Mission District, seemed to bear the brunt of displacement. There was something about the Mission—its location and topography, its mythologized past and imagined future—that made it a magnet for thousands of those moving to San Francisco to be part of the dot-com boom. Standing in the way of this reinvention of the Mission, however, were the many Latina/os, immigrants, and working-class residents already living and working in the neighborhood. Seemingly overnight, longtime Mission District businesses closed and rents doubled. Expensive lofts were built, and upscale restaurants and bars opened—businesses that clearly were not targeted to the longtime residents of the area.

During the most intense periods of gentrification, the common discourse held that displacement, evictions, and new construction were the result of a growing economy and its supposedly uncontrollable need to expand. But there was something else going on as well—another dimension that was not included in the popular narratives on gentrification. Despite the widespread belief that gentrification was "good" for the city, it was not good for the large number of African Americans and Latina/os who were forced out. According to U.S. Census Bureau figures, San Francisco "lost" 25 percent of its African American population and 10 percent of its Latina/o population in the space of five years. In 2000, 60,515 African Americans lived in San Francisco; by 2005, only 45,444 did. The Latina/o population decreased from 109,504 to 98,891 in the same period. Indeed, San Francisco was the only major city in the United States to *lose* Latina/o residents. This loss was even more surprising since the number of new immigrants entering the country as a whole increased by 16 percent from 2000 to 2005, with those from Mexico making up the largest single group.[2]

The forced displacement of African Americans and Latina/os was not part of the popular narrative on gentrification. In a 2006 article, the *San Francisco Chronicle* used census data to report on a "multicultural migration" eastward, but it failed to cite gentrification as a cause.[3] Nor did the article mention that the outmigration of working-class residents to Richmond, Antioch, Tracy, and Stockton has taken them to cities with among the highest rates of foreclosure in the state of California.[4]

If the exodus of people of color was invisible to the mainstream media, it was common knowledge in the city's neighborhoods. Several of the people we interviewed noted the high outmigration of African Americans and Latina/os years before the census data were made public. In an interview in 2000, Conzuelo Tokunaga, who worked with the city-funded Teenage Pregnancy and Parenting Project, told us that a large number of African Americans were leaving San Francisco and moving to Vallejo and Richmond "porque no había oportunidades para ellos" (because there were no opportunities for them). According to Tokunaga, the majority of her

Latina/o clients were also moving to Richmond, where they could find cheaper housing.[5] From the interviews it seemed as though working-class people of color were being pushed out to smaller cities on the fringes of San Francisco, out of sight, yet close enough that they could commute to low-paying jobs downtown.

To the extent that the media discussed outmigration at all, they focused on the positive aspects of moving to the suburbs. In the *San Francisco Chronicle* article, an African American man spoke favorably about moving from Berkeley to Antioch, where kids could attend good schools and families could live in big homes with yards.[6] Unfortunately, many of the low-income people who bought into these outlying communities were left with homes that in time would significantly lose their value. In addition, the subprime mortgages used to purchase these homes resulted in high mortgage payments and, eventually, high foreclosure rates.

For those who stayed in San Francisco, overcrowding was common. Families, friends, and even acquaintances moved in together so they could afford the ever-increasing rents. "Como te digo, comparten una vivienda unifamiliar. Usan hasta la sala. La única área común resulta la cocina y el baño," Tokunaga told us. (Like I said, they share a single-family home. They even use the living room [for sleeping]. The only common areas are the kitchen and bathroom.)[7] As we learned more about the substandard living conditions of populations of color and working-class communities, we wondered who was truly benefiting from gentrification. There was a widespread belief promoted by city politicians, developers, and local media that gentrification was good for San Francisco. Yet we could not help asking: Whom was it good for?

The initial impetus for the "La Misión" project was straightforward: to understand why so many Latina/os were being displaced from the Mission District during the dot-com boom and subsequent bust. As a trained oral historian I used the one tool I knew best, oral historical interviewing and analysis. Methodologically, oral history gave us the tools to understand what people thought, felt, and experienced while their communities were being gentrified—difficult emotions such as fear, longing, desire, regret, and anger. We saw both confusion and clarity. Some residents had no idea of what was happening or how the changes would ultimately affect them. Others pointed only to the positive results and saw themselves as benefiting from gentrification. Still others predicted dire outcomes in terms of what would happen to the Mission District if certain housing, business, and redevelopment policies were not changed.

Most important, oral historical methods helped us examine how Latina/os understood and negotiated a changing geographic, political, and social landscape designed to exclude them. The oral histories consistently revealed Latina/os being displaced at a higher rate than expected. Yet it wasn't until we merged and contextualized the oral histories with policy analysis, urban theory, housing statistics, and economic data that we could demonstrate the full magnitude of the problem.

Telling Stories: Oral History as Practice

> There is no pure authentic, original history. There are only stories, many stories.
> —Emma Pérez, *The Decolonial Imaginary: Writing Chicanas into History*

> So, what do you plan to do with all these stories?
> —Concepcíon "Concha" Mártinez Saucedo, founder, Instituto Familiar de la Raza, 1999

In September 1999 I walked into my Latina/o oral history course ready to teach students how to write testimonios and ethnographies, conduct interviews, and develop a professional oral history. The syllabus had been drafted months earlier, and the carefully selected readings all focused on methodology, theory, and the multiple uses of oral history in different disciplines and populations. When I entered the class, however, I found an unexpected mood in the room. The students were not sitting back waiting for a syllabus and asking whether the books were available at the university bookstore. They were not asking questions about the attendance policy and late papers. Instead, they were unusually quiet, almost reflective.

I interrupted my lecture to find out what was on their minds. It turned out that a number of the students, many of whom were from the Mission District, were being evicted from their homes and losing their jobs. In other cases, it was their family members or friends who had been displaced. The students were concerned about the evictions and about the changing economic and social conditions in the Mission District—the exorbitant rent increases, the building of pricey new condominiums that made it "too expensive to live in the Mission." As each new business, restaurant, and café opened up, my students wondered if they would be the next ones to leave.

We abandoned the syllabus and sketched the initial drafts of a community oral history of gentrification in the Mission District. This was not easy. It was a period when many people were caught up in the chaos, still figuring out what exactly was happening in the neighborhood and how they fit into the equation. By positioning gentrification as the organizing principle, we could interview different communities and groups on the same topic, thereby gaining complex and varying perspectives on displacement. We knew that for some, gentrification was frightening and painful, a death of sorts. For others, it was quite the opposite: it was exciting and full of potential, a rebirth of possibilities. All sides needed to be documented, archived, and told.[8]

We began with a straightforward question: What did we need to know, and whom did we have to interview to learn about gentrification in the Mission District? To organize the project thematically, the students formed groups concerned with specific topics and narrators. For instance, the business group interviewed new business owners, employees of dot-coms, longtime restaurant owners still in business, child care providers, city administrators and planners, and so forth. Once we had found informants, we worked together to develop questions that spoke to them as individuals as well as eliciting their perspectives on gentrification. The idea was to learn more about the individual interviewee while at the same time gathering information on displacement and redevelopment.

Some groups were organized around a theoretical premise or idea. For example, the culture group asked people to define culture and talk about whether it is possible for a neighborhood to have culture. How is culture created, sustained, and used in everyday life? Can culture be lost or erased, and if so how? Many of our interview subjects mentioned *la cultura* as a defining factor in gentrification. A number remarked that we were "losing our culture," that it was being taken away and replaced with something else. We investigated how individuals redefine space to establish shared notions of culture. Could culture be derived from *bodegas*, *mercados*, and *taquerías*? Was it implicit in the murals, in the Latina/o poetry readings, in theater, film festivals, and community events such as Cinco de Mayo and Carnaval? By the same token, could culture be replaced and re-created to suite the interests of a different community or group? If so, how? What were the practices inherent in cultural productions? This group interviewed artists, activists, elders, religious leaders, clergy, academics, police, directors of agencies and nonprofits, gang members, curators, local newspaper reporters, filmmakers, musicians, and organizers of community events such as Cinco de Mayo, Carnaval, and Day of the Dead—anyone who could speak to the question of culture.

By not limiting our ideas of who could talk about gentrification, we learned a great deal about how different communities understand and negotiate neighborhood change. The diversity of informants lent the project a needed depth that challenged notions of essentialism and simplified dichotomies. At times, our subjects expressed what appeared to be contradictory views, agreeing with some aspects of gentrification and resisting others, all in the same interview.

The project, however, included more than interviews. Research, data, and policy analysis were instrumental to the investigation. We did research to prepare for interviews and to contextualize and analyze them afterward. This allowed us to ask narrators important questions and redirect interviews when necessary. We recognized when answers were *not* being given, and we used follow-up questions to help our subjects better explain their answers, demonstrating that we understood the multiple workings of gentrification. This did not always mean that the narrator would be forthcoming. A person's silence and discomfort was enough to signal us to move on. To meet the project's growing need for background information we created a group whose sole task was to conduct research, working closely with local, institutional, and university librarians. Members of the research group were our liaisons to city and state agencies and local newspapers. They identified key figures who could help us understand legal policies, state propositions, and city ordinances.

As we collected the oral histories we were surprised by the different levels of knowledge about gentrification among the narrators, ranging from those who did not understand the term ("Que es gentrificación?") to those who were in a position to influence revitalization policies. Navigating such uneven terrain proved difficult, but we knew that we needed to hear different opinions in order to understand the complexity of gentrification and displacement. Once the interviews were completed and transcribed, we regrouped to share our thoughts and opinions. We discussed what we considered to be critical points of great relevance to the project as well as disappointments and mishaps. It was during these meetings that we debated and decided on general themes and arguments, considering how the results of our interviews informed our understanding of gentrification and its impact on Latina/os. The meetings operated as working groups where we discussed not only the oral histories, as text, but also the theories and methods used in interpreting them.

A persistent question throughout the project was what we intended to do with the oral histories. Who would eventually have access to the stories, and who would control how they could be used in the future? Borrowing from Kristina Minister's analysis of how to construct a feminist frame for oral histories, we were as open and transparent as possible in our interactions with narrators.[9] We explained the project, the reasons for our questions, the issues that we were interested in pursuing, and how their narratives might fit into the whole. We shared information about where the project was headed and what we had already learned, and we let them know where the oral interviews and other materials would be archived.

Although we were committed to the politics of transparency, this did not mean that we encountered no problems or criticisms. We constantly had to negotiate questions about what we planned to do with the oral histories, how we had selected our interviewees, and why we thought recording stories could bring about change. We were asked about our political analysis and positions and our use of certain theoretical and methodological frameworks. Such questions strengthened the project. Yet they also magnified the divide between academic research and community interests, reminding us that much work still needed to be done in the realm of scholar-activism. It was not an easy road to follow, but we had no choice. This was not a project that could be completed in the safety of one's university office.

Putting Oral History into Practice

As the project grew, so did the nagging feeling that it needed to do more. But what? We believed in the importance of "bearing witness and inscribing into history those lived realities that would otherwise succumb to the alchemy of erasure."[10] Yet we wondered if this was enough. It seemed that every day brought more changes to the neighborhood and that local and state governments were doing little to end the massive evictions and displacement of the Latina/o immigrants, artists, activists and cultural workers who called the Mission District home.

It was during this period that we thought about what it meant to put oral history into practice. Could oral histories translate into a larger scholar-activism, or was it enough to document the stories and create an archive to be used in the future? If oral histories were to be used for purposes of activism, what direction would that activism take? Could it operate as part of the academy and still be effective? In documenting and archiving oral histories, we were giving voice and gravity to populations that are often marginalized and lost in the shuffle of gentrification and revitalization. We strongly believed in the power of documentation and voice in making change; in fact, it was the belief in the power of conveying and revealing, of testifying and providing a place for analysis and rethinking, that first inspired the project. Yet we were still left with the dilemma of how to put stories into practice.

In his article on the role of testimonios in the Central American sanctuary movement that arose in the United States during the 1980s, William Westerman argues that hearing testimonios changed how North Americans viewed U.S. policies in Central America, while giving them helped heal the narrators who had endured such horrors. "Testimony is about people rising from a condition of being victims, objects of history, and taking charge of their history, becoming subjects, actors in it. History no longer makes them; they make it, write it, speak it."[11] Westerman effectively summarizes what was critical to our project. In documenting the politics of gentrification, we wanted to provide an alternative reading of displacement. The question, however, was whether to expand our definitions of documentation to include action and participation.

This was both a disturbing and liberating prospect. On the one hand, we were troubled by the notion of the scholar as an outsider who can intervene and leave at will. On the other hand, we were excited by what oral histories and oral historical methodologies might achieve within a proactive and involved context if we allowed ourselves to think differently. We also wondered whether we were expecting too much from oral histories and oral historical methodologies. Was it fair to expect so much? These methodologies have long been used to challenge historical and anthropological theories and methods, to destabilize objectivity, to provide an alternative reading of difference, and to relocate power through voice and documentation. The use of oral history has, as Paul Thompson reminds us, helped establish "a social purpose" to research.[12] It has also, as Renato Rosaldo has demonstrated, allowed us to question objectivity as a methodological premise and incorporate subjectivity, memory, and emotion into our analyses.[13]

Because oral historical theories and methods have the ability to disrupt master narratives, traditional theoretical paradigms, and canonized literary readings of texts, they are commonly used by scholars in ethnic studies, sexuality studies, gender studies, and cultural studies, to name a few. Many of these scholars are interested not only in challenging narrative and text but also in creating a space for an oppositional rethinking of research, form, context, and analysis. In her examination of the relationship between queer theory and oral history, Nan Alamilla Boyd points out that "there are few works in this twenty-five-year-old field that do not depend heavily on oral history methods." At the same time, she argues that queer theory poses a challenge to oral history because "it is nearly impossible for oral history or ethnographic narrators to use language outside the parameters of modern sexual identities. Narrators cannot remove themselves from the discursive practices that create stable subject positions."[14]

In her reading of several foundational and important texts in queer history, Alamilla Boyd notes that while oral history "set the foundation for the production of historical narrative in U.S. gay, lesbian, and queer history," methods were rarely problematized.[15] In many respects, as Alamilla Boyd contends, oral historical methods have not caught up to the multiple needs and demands of queer theory and history, which currently depend on and use oral historical methods for their studies and research. She goes on to argue that instead of expanding and redirecting oral historical theories and methods, it may be necessary instead to reconstitute their uses and practices so that they can better operate within a larger, more complicated, and ever-changing discourse.

While we echoed Alamilla Boyd's call to complicate oral history analysis and method, we were still left with the divide between process and action. Were we, as a result of paradigmatic limitations, at risk of being perpetually stuck in process? At the same time, was it "our place" to move into action? It was a theoretical and methodological dilemma that demanded the inclusion and incorporation of community members and residents who were critical to redefining the project and its uses. A central objective of many involved in the project was to employ the oral histories in a constructive way. While many saw the utility in archiving the oral histories, others wanted the oral histories, policy papers, sources, and printed media to be used to change policies, organize communities, and foster collaborations. We decided to do both. The project materials would be open and available to anyone interested in the topic.

Although it was not easy, we learned to develop fluid, undefined spaces where different communities, including professors, students, artists, and members of nonprofit and activist organizations, could participate in producing knowledge and sharing authority.[16] Many of our participants attended and spoke at supervisor meetings, became members of the Mission Anti-Displacement Coalition, wrote letters and opinion pieces protesting gentrification for publication in the local newspaper, and organized community brown-bags and talks. Others used the oral histories and sources to create art and develop a website where the oral histories could be posted online. The varied collaborations changed our thinking about interpretation, process, and practice. They magnified the different ways in which oral histories are understood within the community and the role of documentation and archives in making change.

Documenting the Undocumented: The Politics and Process of Latina/o Oral Histories

> I have lived in the Mission for the last twenty years and it has never been so unfamiliar to me as it is right now. I remember this neighborhood being called a ghetto because it was cheap to live here, it was dirty, and there was violence. Never once did I believe it would be trendy or the new Silicon Valley.
> —Jennifer Aparicio, Mission District resident, 2000

> Opposition to gentrification here and now can too quickly be dismissed as a hunter-gatherer rejection of "progress." In fact, for those impoverished, evicted or made homeless in its wake, gentrification is indeed a dirty word and it should stay a dirty word.
> —Neil Smith, *The New Urban Frontier: Gentrification and the Revanchist City*

In his seminal work on oral history, Paul Thompson argues that oral sources have the ability to capture and convey the immediacy of a moment and to explain events as they take place.[17] For Alessandro Portelli, what makes oral histories so valuable is that they tell us "not just what people did, but what they wanted to do, what they believed they were doing, and what they now think they did."[18] Both illustrate how oral history methods can emphasize the present while never losing sight of recollection and memory. Furthermore, oral histories can also provide glimpses into possibility, longing, and the future. This allows subjects to reconsider their beliefs, change their minds, and reassess their thoughts, even at the very moment of recounting their experiences. The oral historical method does not assume that people continue to think in the same way; it accepts that events, people, actions, belief systems, scholarship, and fiction, to name a few, have the power to change how people think and respond to the world around them. There are few historical methods that account for and encourage such fluidity and shifts. Unlike traditional historical narratives, where source and text can be stagnant and facts can seem indisputable, oral history depends on movement and on the recognition that facts can be interpreted differently by different narrators.

Theoretical movement and imprecise narratives became particularly important when we interviewed immigrants, undocumented migrants, the homeless, and temporary residents. These interviews highlighted the need to disrupt fixed notions of space and location, especially when discussing the politics of property, ownership, and access. In 2000, 50 percent of the Mission District's population was Latina/o, compared to just 14 percent for the city as a whole. The Mission also had an extremely high percentage of renters, 82 percent, compared to the citywide average of 65 percent. Among the Latina/o population of the Mission District, 73 percent were renters and 27 percent owned their homes. With such a large Latina/o population in the neighborhood and nearly three-quarters of them in rental units, eviction and displacement from the Mission hit Latina/os particularly hard.[19]

However, the Latina/o population is not monolithic, and immigration status played a larger role than expected in how our Latina/o informants articulated their sense of space. Undocumented and first-generation immigrants did not have the same degree of attachment to neighborhood space as did second-, third-, and fourth-generation residents. Undocumented and first-generation migrants were more likely to see themselves as temporary residents in reinvented communities. Although they recognized the utility of living and working in a Latina/o neighborhood where they could speak Spanish, buy familiar products, and establish important informal networks, they showed little attachment to the Mission District as a neighborhood. Most considered their families and friends back home to be their primary community. They identified with their countries of origin and tended to see community in the United States as something that could be continuously remade.

By contrast, Latina/o informants who were born in the United States or had arrived at a very young age had a deeper collective historical memory of the Mission District as a distinctly Latina/o community. They were quick to cite political and cultural events, family ties, and their experiences in schools, churches, jobs, and even gangs as examples of what defined them as being from "La Misión." They were the most vocal in challenging and resisting gentrification, as they considered it a direct threat to their neighborhood. Many of their memories were inherited, with interviewees citing the borrowed recollections of their parents, neighbors, and friends who had immigrated years ago. They remembered the businesses they frequented as children, where everyone spoke Spanish and where you could hang out for hours and "nobody cared because you were like family." They talked about getting married and raising their families in the same neighborhood they had grown up in. They told stories about Precita Park and how it "used to be" when they hung out at the park and "just made music." Others remembered driving up and down Mission Street in their lowriders, meeting friends, and ending up at Dolores Park. Some discussed their involvement in founding the Mission Cultural Center for Latino Arts, Galería de la Raza, or Precita Eyes Mural Center, or being part of the Mujeres Muralistas.

In addition to transcribing memories, we also translated experience. A number of our narrators, longtime residents as well as new immigrants, spoke Spanish. Some mixed Spanish words with English and others used Spanish words to emphasize a point or establish an intimate rapport with the person interviewing them. This demanded that we not only translate words and meanings but also examine how language influences perspective and memories. Because many of the interviewers were Latina/os or students in the Latina/o oral history course, or both, Spanish was used to create familiarity and trust between subject and interviewer. In cases where an interviewer could not speak Spanish, there seemed to be some hesitancy on the part of some subjects to reveal certain thoughts and recollections. At such times, narrators might revert to a more formal interview style, using less anecdotal language and carefully explaining their thoughts and experiences to help the interviewer understand them. At times, the stories being told were painful to both the narrators and the interviewers. From roughly 1997 to 2000, over 1,000 Latina/o families were displaced from the Mission District.[20] The dramatic rise in evictions and displacement from the Mission left many confused and shocked.

In the early stages of the project we had not yet learned of the devastating effects of two key policies: the Ellis Act and Owner Move-In. Both were remarkably efficient in evicting thousands from their homes. The Ellis Act allows landlords to evict tenants in order to convert rental units to ownership units, such as condos. "Owner move-in," also known as owner occupancy, allows evictions so that the landlord can occupy the building. A few years later, when the numbers were made public, we learned that the majority of evictions in the city took place under one or the other of these policies.

Ellis Act and owner move-in evictions tripled between 1996 and 1998.[21] In his study of gentrification in the Mission District, Simon Velazquez Alejandrino states that owner move-ins "accounted for roughly a third of all evictions in San Francisco in 1999 alone, and were by far the most common type of eviction in the city." In the same year, 16 percent San Francisco's evictions were attributed to the Ellis Act. Fourteen percent of Ellis Act evictions in 1999 occurred in the Mission District, even though the Mission has only 9 percent of the city's rental units.[22] By researching housing and rental policies, we came to understand what our interviewers meant when they mentioned getting notices demanding that they move out so that owners could make repairs or move into the units themselves.

Liliana González recounted that slowly everybody around her "started to move away."[23] She remembered how her landlord, intent on making a profit during the boom time, evicted her family from the apartment where she had lived for most of her life. The eviction broke up her family, as some members ended up living in the East Bay and others in San Francisco. Her father left the Bay Area altogether and moved back to El Salvador where he was born. We underestimated the level of fear, rage, and sadness surrounding evictions and displacement. We also realized that narrators self-edited and left things out as a way to control their stories and perhaps even protect themselves from the pain of further exposure. It was as though when they heard themselves speak out loud, it made their situation even more real. We accepted the fragmented memories, the deliberate silences, the unwillingness to answer questions or expand, and the many digressions as valued text. It wasn't always what people said, but *how* they said it. Body language, tone of voice, facial expressions, and posture spoke volumes and helped us understand the politics of language, authority, power, and space. This was particularly helpful in discussions that touched on language and immigration status.

Although we were conscious that we were asking our subjects to discuss sensitive topics, we also knew that not all would respond in the same way. Some narrators trusted the interviewers and were willing to explore painful emotions. Others demanded to see the questions beforehand, answering only those they felt comfortable with. It was important to recognize that this too was part of the narration; it was all part of the telling.

After the interviews we would gather together and share what we had learned. Often, the interviewers reported that informants had taken them on walks, showing them the houses from which family, friends, and neighbors had been evicted, as well as the construction of new and expensive housing they could not afford. These physical manifestations of displacement became part of the oral histories, illustrating narratives of loss. It was reminiscent of Westerman's claim that "testimony can be visual too." When he asked a Central American refugee to provide him with a testimonio, the man "pulled up his sleeve to reveal a deep gouged out scar from a bullet wound in his shoulder."[24] We too were being asked to see scars. I went on my share of walks. I accompanied subjects as they showed me where murals had been whitewashed, where they had been arrested for loitering, where stores used to stand, and where they used to live and work.

Those involved in gentrifying the community also took us on walks. But these were celebratory, almost exuberant walks, filled with a narrative of possibility. These subjects appeared impervious to the destruction of houses, businesses, and nonprofits that had once occupied the sites on which they were now rebuilding. In her reflection on an interview she conducted with an owner of several businesses in the Mission District, Jennifer Aparicio explained that the subject had showed her different construction sites, describing his vision for the future of Mission Street. He had proudly noted that a certain very expensive restaurant, one that he owned, was being built where "an old bargain outlet" once stood. He seemed unaware that the residents who most needed such an outlet could never afford to eat at the restaurant he was building.[25]

"Whiteness as Property": Gentrification and the Uses of Whiteness

> Only white possession and occupation of land was validated and therefore privileged as a basis for property rights. The distinct forms of exploitation each contributed in varying ways to the construction of whiteness as property.
> —Cheryl L. Harris, *Whiteness as Property*

> There's a different mix of people coming in and out now. Got a lot of Caucasian people in and out of the Mission which you never actually, you know, seen. I mean we got people walking around at like two or three in the morning in places that you know me, myself, and my group wouldn't go to a few years ago.
> —Jason Espinoza, Mission District resident, 2004

As we conducted oral histories, gathered data, and archived sources, we realized that there was a common thread in many of the interviews and much of the research—the workings of whiteness. Whiteness and/or "white people" were often referred to as the reason why changes were "happening to our community." Many of the subjects commented on the large numbers of white people moving into the area, the opening of businesses that seemed to cater to white customers, and the impact whiteness had in transforming the culture of the neighborhood. A familiar refrain in the interviews was that the Mission District was "just not the same anymore."

In his oral history, José Daniel Cruz Solis, a young resident, discussed how people of color and whites were treated differently when occupying the same spaces in the Mission District.

> I remember it was cool to walk down the street really late at night. But then it became—you know. Cops were coming every night harassing people of color and telling them, "Oh, it's too late for you to be out on the street." But when it was white folks, I never saw that they [the cops] approached them, you know what I mean? So that's definitely something that I noticed.[26]

For Solis, the change in treatment, from being free to walk the streets late at night to being harassed, informed his experience of gentrification as a process that restricted the movement of brown bodies in urban space. It revealed how whiteness influences and redefines who can "safely" occupy space. Solis's contention of disparate treatment is borne out by the record of city ordinances and policies aimed at restricting the movements of people of color. These include curfews, prosecution of taggers, and gang injunctions, which limit the spatial areas that gang members can access and occupy.

Later in the interview, Solis expressed his surprise at seeing white people walking in parts of the neighborhood where he himself, "a lifelong member of the Mission District," would never go late at night. His notion of permissible physical movement was influenced by a memory of neighborhood spaces that designated some areas as safe and others as dangerous. But this understanding was not shared by others new to the Mission. They lacked Solis's geographic memory and shared history and as a result they moved about the neighborhood as they pleased, with no apparent awareness of violence or danger. Solis's interview initiates a dialogue on whether white bodies can actually make dangerous spaces safe simply by accessing those spaces and privileging whiteness.

We also conducted interviews with new restaurant and business owners, who lacked the historical memory of location so commonly expressed by long-term residents. They spent little time ruminating about the past or about how new developments were encroaching on and changing the neighborhood. Indeed, they considered their actions in opening new businesses to be good for the community, because they were providing jobs to

Mission District residents and making the streets safer for everyone. The expensive housing units and upscale restaurants would attract wealthier residents and clientele, which in turn would make the neighborhood better for everyone. Yet some of the new entrepreneurs appeared to be aware that their rosy view was not widely shared. The majority who gave interviews did so on condition that they not be published without their written consent. Of all of our interviews, the ones with business and restaurant owners moving into the Mission District, those most responsible for gentrifying the neighborhood, were the most restricted.[27]

The discourse on whiteness and location was complicated, tangled, and at times muted when it came to property ownership and entitlement to space. It was frustrating to see such a deviation in experience. Those who questioned gentrification provided examples of how displacement had affected them or someone they knew. One of the more emotionally difficult aspects of the project was witnessing long-term residents realize, often as they were telling their oral histories, that what they had previously used to define someone as "from the Mission" (history, family, culture, traditions) no longer held true. At the height of the housing boom, it seemed that what conferred belonging, the real test of power, was property ownership and access to space—a process marked and defined by whiteness.

In her work on the multiple uses of whiteness among Latina/os in Chicago, Ana Y. Ramos-Zayas comments on the relationship between region and race, noting that locality is a "critical actor in the production and reproduction of a powerful language of social difference and racial formations or racialization." She goes on to argue that the "mutations of urban spaces and cultural orders are interpreted through various contours of whiteness, a term which refers to the cultural web of assumptions of normality and invisibility that maintains the social privileges, power, and hierarchies typically associated with white skin."[28] By extending her analysis to space, Ramos-Zayas traces how whiteness, as a production and process, normalizes privilege and entitlement to urban space and is implicit in lessening and even erasing Latina/o access to that space. Ramos-Zayas further complicates her study by showing how different Latina/o groups gauge and use varying definitions of whiteness to understand neighborhood change. Using interviews and first-person accounts, Ramos-Zayas notes how Latina/os differentiated whites moving into the area—*los blancos* or *los americanos*—from ethnic whites who had lived and worked for many years in neighborhoods that were once predominantly Polish, German, or Irish. Interestingly, while some Latina/os were critical of gentrification, others saw those changes as part of a larger white mobility that had the potential to serve their interests as well.

In her analysis of whiteness as property, legal scholar Cheryl Harris argues that whiteness historically has been embedded in the ways that space is eventually configured and used. She contends that whiteness as a practice is defined by private property and that "the origins of property rights in the United States are rooted in racial domination."[29] Harris's intervention was important in moving past the concept of whiteness as racialized identity to an understanding of whiteness as a historical practice that explains entitlement and access to space. Gentrification did not create the uses of whiteness; it replicated and reified a politics and policy that were already part of historical conceptions and definitions of property in the United States.

This idea was key to understanding the frequent use of terminology such as "urban pioneers" and "urban homesteaders" by real estate agents and developers. Such terms romanticize and fetishize white investors buying into communities of color. As Neil Smith argues, "In the language of gentrification, the appeal to frontier imagery has been exact: urban pioneers, urban homesteaders and urban cowboys became the new folk heroes of the urban frontier." Smith further explains how the "arrogant" metaphor of the pioneer, laden with racist colonial connotations, was taken to its most absurd extreme in the 1980s when "real estate magazines even talked about 'urban scouts' whose job it was to scout out the flanks of gentrifying neighborhoods, check the landscape for profitable reinvestment, and, at the same time, to report home about how friendly the natives were."[30]

Colonial imagery and practices were also evident in the rush to rename neighborhoods. Over the last ten years, real estate agents, developers, and businesses have carved out and renamed sections of San Francisco neighborhoods in an attempt to both erase their racialized past and *whiten* their potential future. This practice has been quite effective. At the moment, there are over one hundred different neighborhoods in San Francisco, a city that measures only forty-nine square miles.[31]

Unraveling Parallel Discourses: Scripting Displacement

The change kicked off when the Valencia Gardens projects (so crime-ridden, they seemed straight out of *The Wire*) were razed in 2004 and replaced by a public-housing development of modern flats and town-houses. With the streets suddenly safer, the hood attracted a handful of new businesses, including Mission Beach Cafe, indie clothing shop

Miranda Caroligne, and, most recently, super-sleek Conduit, which draws diners from all over the city. Some blocks still feel ignored, but these new spots—along with art-gallery openings and neighborhood anchor Zeitgeist—are keeping the streets abuzz after dark.
—Marcia Gagliardi, "From Projects to Prosciutto," *San Francisco*, May 2008

So, welcome to el barrio. You may enjoy it. I may have to leave, too bad. But I am not really worried. It was getting weird anyway. All these espresso and bagels, vegetarian burritos and organic foods I can't afford. Oh well, maybe next time, when Willie Brown comes down, the City Hall will be able to save the money on the Spanish banners. By then, we may be all gone. As you gringos say, adios, amigo!
—"Welcome to the Mission District: Gentrification and Overcrowding," *Street Sheet*, May 18, 2004

During the height of the dot-com boom, local newspapers, magazines, and reviews cheered the transformation of the "once seedy" Mission District to a trendy neighborhood where one could eat in expensive restaurants and shop in hip boutiques. Upscale magazines, like the glossy *San Francisco* magazine, applauded each new business and building as a step forward in revitalizing the community and making it safe for anyone to visit or live in the Mission District.

The language of safety was tied to a diffused and nuanced articulation of race and danger. Employing terms such as *gritty*, *shady*, and *sketchy* to denote racialized populations and spaces as violent, reporters and reviewers heralded a transformation whose success rested on erasing all elements of race, ethnicity, culture, immigration, and difference, except for those that gave the neighborhood its "character." In addition to recording what people thought about gentrification, we wanted to investigate why, in a neighborhood where Latina/os made up 50 percent of the population, they were constantly silenced and erased from mainstream media and public discourse. They simply did not exist.

In 2000 the Bay Area lost an estimated 50,000 residents because they could no longer afford to live there.[32] This forced population exodus did not keep the mainstream media from celebrating the development of "restaurant row" on Valencia Street, the opening of trendy boutiques and bars, and the costly, damaging work/live loft conversions in the Inner Mission. The articles read as a collective sigh of relief, expressing an over-riding sense that it was now okay to live in the Mission. It was no longer a place go slumming in dicey neighborhood bars, taquerías, and dollar stores. The Mission District was changing, and for all the *right* reasons.

This overwhelmingly positive discourse on gentrification rested uncomfortably with the oral historical narratives we collected at the time. It was as though different communities were operating in parallel universes that had nothing to do with each other. It was up to the local independent newspapers, including the *Mission News*, the bilingual *El Tecolote*, and the *Bay Guardian*, to report on evictions and displacement.

Understanding the overwhelming support for gentrification was further complicated by San Francisco's half-century history of redevelopment and revitalization.[33] Was the current period of intense gentrification, fueled by the dot-com boom, distinct from the others, or was it the same, just packaged and articulated differently? From our research, it was evident that gentrification in San Francisco followed a pattern similar to that in other major cities and that it was clearly deliberate. Yet the assumptions that it was unplanned and unstoppable persisted, despite evidence to the contrary.

The fear and anxiety expressed in the interviews was, unfortunately, warranted. San Francisco has a long history of displacing poor, working-class populations of color to serve the interests of wealth and capital production. Tracing the relationship between race and urban development in San Francisco, Chester Hartman shows that the exclusion of populations of color in favor of whites has been a consistent and intentional feature of redevelopment. In the late 1950s, this process focused on the South of Market area. City officials, Hartman says, were concerned about "the changing face of San Francisco into a 'city of color,' with increasing African, Asian, and Latino populations" living close to the economic center of the city. Developers and local politicians, including Mayor Christopher George, saw this as a major obstacle to attracting corporate investors and developers. This problem, it seemed, could be solved by redevelopment. "Urban renewal could be used to displace the city's minorities and recapture the centrally located residential areas they had inherited after whites moved out."[34]

Renewal projects sprang up throughout the city, the most notorious being the Fillmore Redevelopment Project, which began in 1953 and formally ended in 2001. During the 1960s and '70s, when the Fillmore Redevelopment A-1 and A-2 projects were in full swing, an estimated 60 percent of African Americans in the city lost their homes and businesses and were eventually forced to leave. To mitigate the large displacement of African Americans—and counter the negative press and growing resentment in the African American community—the San Francisco Redevelopment Agency created a Certificate of Preference that would allow home and business owners to return to the Fillmore District after it was rebuilt. However, because it took the Redevelopment Agency so long to complete the project, most people had no choice but to move elsewhere. So far, only 4 percent of the return certificates have been used. As of this writing, the African American neighborhoods of Bayview and Hunter Points are facing intense and entrenched redevelopment battles.

Attempting to Conclude

> Speaking in gentrification terms, the part of the Mission between Duboce Avenue and 16th Street is a bit of a late bloomer: The wave of hipsterdom that flooded upper Valencia and Guerrero Streets during the last ten years pretty much stopped at 16th. But now foodies and culturephiles, presumably tired of the Mission hype—and looking for a new sketchy neighborhood to demarginalize—are moving in.
> —Marcia Gagliardi, "From Projects to Prosciutto," *San Francisco*, May 2008

> Spaces are not neutral.
> —Mary Pat Brady, *Extinct Lands, Temporal Geographies: Chicana Literature and the Urgency of Space*

Despite the dot-com bust, the subprime mortgage collapse, the high unemployment rates, and the bailouts of major banks, the gentrification of San Francisco continues.[35] In May 2008 *San Francisco* magazine ran a brief article titled "From Projects to Prosciutto," with a revealing subtitle: "A pass-through neighborhood on the north end of the Mission is finally giving people a reason to stop and look around." What makes Marcia Gagliardi's article of particular interest are the words and images used to describe gentrification. Gagliardi's enthusiastic call that there is more to gentrify, that ten years after the start of gentrification there are still "sketchy" neighborhoods to demarginalize, expresses a deep sense of privilege and entitlement to space.

What is missing from Gagliardi's reading of the Mission District is any consciousness of the large community of people who still live and work there. Latina/os are never mentioned or discussed as part of the community. The prevailing notion, perhaps even fantasy, is that those Latina/os who remain will eventually leave, making the area "truly safe" and completing the process of gentrification. But there are no indications that Latina/os will leave the community for good. Latina/os are still here, working, buying groceries, raising children, going to school, reading poetry, and participating in the everyday life of the Mission District—even if Gagliardi chooses to ignore them.

In the spring of 2009 the students in my Latina/o oral history class launched another oral history project, this one tracing the workings of poverty. In 2010, California, along with Nevada and Michigan, led the country in unemployment and foreclosure rates, with an estimated 12.4 percent of Californians out of work. In the state of California, Latina/os experienced the highest rate of foreclosures of any group, with an estimated 48 percent of foreclosures tied to Latina/o borrowers.[36] This time, when I asked the class whether they knew anyone who had lost a job, every hand in a class of fifty students shot up. When I asked them whether they knew someone who had lost or was losing a home, over half raised their hands. That was enough to motivate us to embark on another oral history community project. We have no idea where this project will take us, but we are ready to listen, learn, make more mistakes, and in the end, tell the stories that have yet to be told.

Notes

Thank you to Teresa Barnett and Chon Noriega for inviting me to be part of this book project, to Rebecca Frazier for her assistance, and to the anonymous readers for their helpful comments and suggestions. I am thankful to everyone involved in the community oral history project, especially those who so generously provided us with their oral histories. This article is dedicated to my good friend Warren Yee, who after thirty years of telling stories and running the Lexington Market on Bush Street was forced, as a result of gentrification, to close his store and leave the neighborhood.

Epigraphs. Elizabeth Kostova, *The Historian* (New York: Little, Brown, 2005), xv; Rosario Anaya, interview by Roberto Eligio Alfaro for "La Misión: Voices of Resistance" project, 1999; Jennifer Aparicio, "The Changing Mission: A Restaurant Owner's Perspective," written for "La Misión: Voices of Resistance" project, 2000; conversation with Concepción Martínez Saucedo, founder and director of Instituto Familiar de la Raza, Mission District, 1999; "Welcome to the Mission District: Gentrification and Overcrowding," *Street Sheet* (a San Francisco street newspaper focusing on poverty and housing), May 18, 2004; Neil Smith, *The New Urban Frontier: Gentrification and the Revanchist City* (New York: Routledge, 1996), 34; Marcia Gagliardi, "From Projects to Prosciutto," *San Francisco*, May 2008, 72–73; Jason Espinoza, interview by Nicole Espinosa for "La Misión: Voices of Resistance" project, 2004; Gagliardi, "From Projects to Prosciutto," 72–73.

1. See Nancy Raquel Mirabal, "Geographies of Displacement: Latina/os, Oral History, and the Politics of Gentrification in San Francisco's Mission District," *Public Historian: A Journal of Public History* 31, no. 2 (May 2009).

2. Figures are from the 2000 U.S. Census and the Census Bureau's 2005 American Community Survey. The city's total population in 2005 was 719,077.

3. Leslie Fulbright and Janine DeFao, "The Bay Area's Minority Migration; Population Shift: Inner Cities Shrinking as Nonwhites Seek Better Schools and Lives," *San Francisco Chronicle*, August 15, 2006.

4. Cities located east of San Francisco and in the Central Valley have been hardest hit by the housing crash, with Modesto, Merced, and Stockton having the highest share of housing units in foreclosure. Debbie Gruenstein Bocian et al., *Dreams Deferred: Impacts and Characteristics of the California Foreclosure Crisis*, Oakland, CA: Center for Responsible Lending, August 2010.

5. Conzuelo Tokunaga, interview by Sonia Lucana for La Misión: Voices of Resistance project, 2000.

6. Fulbright and DeFao, "The Bay Area's Minority Migration."

7. Conzuelo Tokunaga, interview by Sonia Lucana, 2000.

8. An integral part of the project was choice. Not everyone in the oral history class participated in the project. Students could carry out oral histories that were not about gentrification. Students who did participate were given full ownership of their interviews and final projects, even if they chose *not* to include them in the overall project. Each student who was involved in the class project was individually credited with conducting his or her interviews and acknowledged as the principal oral historian for those interviews. All publications, talks, and public use of the interviews must cite that student as the oral historian.

9. Kristina Minister, "A Feminist Frame for the Oral History Interview," in *Women's Words: The Feminist Practice of Oral History*, ed. Sherna Berger Gluck and Daphne Patai (New York: Routledge, 1991). Also see Juanita Johnson-Bailey, "The Ties that Bind and the Shackles that Separate: Race, Gender, Class, and Color in a Research Process," *International Journal of Qualitative Studies in Education* 12, no. 6 (November 1999): 659–70; and Tami Spry, "Performing Autoethnography: An Embodied Methodological Praxis," *Qualitative Inquiry* 7, no. 6 (2001): 706–32.

10. Latina Feminist Group, *Telling to Live: Latina Feminist Testimonios* (Durham, NC: Duke University Press, 2001), 2

11. William Westerman, "Central American Refugee Testimonies and Performed Life Histories," in *The Oral History Reader*, ed. Robert Perks and Alistair Thomson, 230 (New York: Routledge, 1998).

12. Paul Thompson, *The Voice of the Past: Oral History* (New York: Oxford University Press, 2000)

13. Renato Rosaldo, *Culture and Truth: The Remaking of Social Analysis* (Boston: Beacon Press, 1989).

14. Nan Alamilla Boyd, "Who Is the Subject? Queer Theory Meets Oral History," *Journal of the History of Sexuality* 17, no. 2 (May 2008): 180. Also see Arnaldo Cruz-Malavé, *Queer Latino Testimonio, Keith Haring, and Juanito Xtravaganza: Hard Tails* (New York: Palgrave Macmillan, 2007)

15. Alamilla Boyd, "Who Is the Subject?" 180.

16. See Michael Frisch, *A Shared Authority: Essays on the Craft and Meaning of Oral and Public History* (Albany: State University of New York Press, 1990).

17. Thompson, *Voice of the Past*, 2000.

18. Alessandro Portelli, "What Makes Oral History Different," in Perks and Thomson, *Oral History Reader*, 67.

19. These statistics, based on 2000 U.S. Census data, are discussed in two reports published by the Mission Economic Development Agency (MEDA) in San Francisco, "Socio-Economic Profile of the Mission District" (2006) and Simon Velasquez Alejandrino, "Gentrification in San Francisco's Mission District: Indicators and Policy Recommendations" (2000).

20. Beatriz Johnston Hernández, "The Invaders: An Out-of-Control Influx of Dot-Commers Is Displacing San Francisco's Latino Neighborhood," *El Andar* (Santa Cruz, CA), Fall 2000, 55.

21. According to Daniel Zoll, owner move-in evictions rose from 433 in 1996 to 1,253 in 1998. "The Economic Cleansing of San Francisco: Is San Francisco Becoming the First Fully Gentrified City in America?" *San Francisco Bay Guardian*, October 7, 1998.

22. Velasquez Alejandrino, "Gentrification in San Francisco's Mission District," 20–22. The owner move-in policy allows an owner to evict a tenant if the owner resides in the building for thirty-six months following the eviction. After this period, the owner can return the unit to the rental market. Because the San Francisco's rent control ordinance only applies to occupied units and sets no rent restrictions on newly vacated units, the landlord can rerent the unit at market rate. Tenant advocates have argued that landlords use owner move-in evictions to escape rent control. The Ellis Act, passed by the state of California in 1986, allows property owners to evict tenants in order to remove all of their properties from the rental market. Owners must give tenants first right of refusal if the unit is returned to the rental market. Owners must also pay $4,500 to low-income tenants and $3,000 to elderly or disabled tenants who are evicted under the Act.

23. Liliana González, interview by Alberto Espinosa for La Misión: Voices of Resistance project, 1999.

24. Westerman, "Central American Refugee Testimonies and Performed Life Histories," 230.

25. Jon Varnedoe, interview by Jennifer Aparicio for La Misión: Voices of Resistance project, 2000.

26. José Daniel Cruz Solis, interview by Isabel Pulido for La Misión: Voices of Resistance project, 1999.

27. Included in all release forms were directions for how the interview can and should be used. Narrators have ultimate control of their interviews, and we agreed not to publish, quote, or cite any interview without the narrator's approval. Of all of the subjects interviewed, new business owners were the least likely to give us permission to use their interviews.

28. Ana Ramos-Zayas, "All This Is Turning White Now: Latino Construction of 'White Culture' and Whiteness in Chicago," *Centro: Journal of the Center for Puerto Rican Studies* 13, no. 2 (Fall 2001): 74.

29. Cheryl L. Harris, "Whiteness as Property," *Harvard Law Review* 106, no. 8 (June 1993): 1716.

30. Neil Smith, *The New Urban Frontier: Gentrification and the Revanchist City* (New York: Routledge Press, 1996), xiv.

31. Information and statistics provided by the San Francisco Visitor's Bureau have been very helpful in understanding how San Francisco's image has been packaged for consumption. For example, the Western Addition, a historically African American and Japanese American community, has recently been renamed NoPa (North of the Panhandle), even though it is not geographically located north of the Panhandle park. Similar renamings include the Tendernob, an area between the Tenderloin and Nob Hill; NoMa, the area north of Market Street; and Hayes Valley. And of course, there are the different parts of the Mission District, including Upper and Lower Mission, Mission Terrace, TransMission, and Mission Heights.

32. Kelly Zito, "Expanding or Ready to Burst?" *San Francisco Chronicle*, May 26, 2000.

33. In the 1950s the San Francisco Board of Supervisors and the mayor created an urban renewal program to expand the downtown area and revitalize parts of the city, including the Fillmore District, which at the time had a large African American population. In 1959 he had become executive director of the San Francisco Redevelopment Agency, and within twenty years he had displaced thousands of poor, working-class African Americans. Under his leadership the San Francisco Redevelopment Agency became what Chester Hartman has characterized as a "powerful and aggressive army out to capture as much downtown land as it could: not only the Golden Gateway and South of Market but also Chinatown, the Tenderloin (a decidedly not upscale area north of Market), and the port." Hartman explains that under the "rubric of 'slum clearance' and 'blight removal,' the agency turned to systematically sweeping out the poor, with the full backing of the city's power elite." Chester Hartman with Sarah Carnochan, *City for Sale: The Transformation of San Francisco* (Berkeley: University of California Press, 2002), 19. Although the city government and the planning department reassured community members that they would not lose their homes or properties, African Americans were forced to sell their homes and businesses to make way for the expansion of streets and commercial areas. For those who lost their homes, compensation was minimal, forcing many to choose either to live in the housing projects being built or to move out of the city altogether. African American activists labeled the redevelopment of the Fillmore as "no more Fillmore." See also Gray Brechin, *Imperial San Francisco: Urban Power, Earthly Ruin* (Berkeley: University of California Press, 1999).

34. Hartman, *City for Sale*, 17.

35. A recent development proposal is the Eastern Neighborhoods Community Plan. Its aim is to set new zoning policies and funding levels for development of the eastern part of San Francisco, which includes the Mission District, eastern SoMa (South of Market), Potrero Hill, and the Central Waterfront. This contentious proposal led to a fight between developers and anti-gentrification forces such as the Mission Anti-Displacement Coalition, the South of Market Community Action Network, and the Potrero Boosters Neighborhood Association. In the

Bayview District, a predominantly African American, working-class neighborhood, debates over "valuable property" have followed on the heels of the Third Street rail line, a 5.1-mile extension of light rail service into one of the most disenfranchised communities in San Francisco. This has dramatically altered the profile of the neighborhood and has made it an area where middle-class families want to live and invest. See Steven T. Jones and Maria Dinzeo, "Moment of Truth: The Eastern Neighborhoods Plan Could Determine Whether San Francisco Retains Its Working-class Residents," *San Francisco Bay Guardian*, September 10–16, 2008.

36. Gruenstein Bocian et al., *Dreams Deferred*.

"It Wasn't a Sweet Life"

Engaging Students in Oral History Interviewing across Race, Class, and Generations

Susan D. Rose

> I've studied here for almost four years and I had no idea what kind
> of community lay just two blocks from campus—and I never would
> have, had it not been for this course. I have met some wonderful,
> amazing people.
> —Jesse Morrell, Dickinson College student

Dickinson College is a small, predominantly white liberal arts college
located in Carlisle, a small town in south-central Pennsylvania. Like many
historically white American colleges and universities, Dickinson faces the
challenge of how to engage its primarily white students—and an increasing number of African, Latino, Asian, and Native American (ALANA)
students—in meaningful dialogues about diversity.[1] The college is known
for encouraging its students to study abroad, and it has worked actively over
the past decade to diversity its faculty and student body. The percentage
of students of color has risen from 5 percent to 16 percent. The college
continues to search for effective ways to create an intellectual community that prepares all of its members to live creatively, productively, and
harmoniously in a multicultural society and world. This cannot be done
simply by making the campus demographically more diverse or by sending
students to foreign countries. Rather, the institution must intentionally
engage diversity in ways that create greater understanding and empathy
and thereby enrich the entire campus and its surrounding community.

I am on the sociology faculty at the college, and for us a key strategy
has been to look beyond the campus to the town. Dickinson is located in

the borough of Carlisle, Pennsylvania, which is the county seat of Cumberland County. In 2000 the borough had 17,970 residents, 14 percent of whom live at or below poverty level. Among African American residents, one-third live below poverty level. By contrast, nearly 40 percent of Dickinson students come from private school backgrounds, and a majority grew up in households whose median income is easily quadruple that of Carlisle residents. While African Americans make up only 6.9 percent of the borough population, they have deep roots in Carlisle, dating back to the Revolutionary era. And the heart of the town's black community is located just two blocks from the Dickinson campus.[2]

We have found that collaborative fieldwork and oral history interviewing under the applied sociological framework of community studies has been an effective way of connecting students with the town, and particularly with the town's African American community. In 1989–90 we launched a two-stage oral history project called the "Smalltown" project. Students and faculty worked in research teams with community members to collect multigenerational oral histories that revealed the origins and continuing development of the local African American community. This interracial college-community collaboration helped our students get to know their neighbors and better understand town-gown relations. It also yielded an important study of change and continuity in race relations in twentieth-century small-town America.

For Carlisle's African Americans, the project provided a way to document and validate their history. For Dickinson students, the process of interviewing black town residents taught them much about race and class relations, family and gender, education, work, housing, leisure, and religion in an ostensibly "white" town. It also taught them about themselves. At first, thinking their task was to document the experiences of African Americans, students did not realize that they were also going to be exploring the experience of growing up white, both at the turn of the century and today. Perhaps most important, the students overcame their fear of entering into authentic conversations with other people whose lives seemed quite different from their own. They became active listeners. For their part, community members came to know students as diverse individuals rather than just as "the rich kids down the street." Challenging stereotypes on both sides, participants in the oral history project came to appreciate the multidimensionality of those once considered strangers.

Listening to African American Narratives in a Predominantly White Town

The team that came together for the first stage of the project in 1989–90 was composed of four African Americans (a minister, a sixth-grade teacher, and two high school students) and five whites (an eleventh-grade English teacher, two college professors including me, and two college students). Our various concerns included race relations in the town, discrimination in the local school system, the marginalization of the African American community, and the isolation of Dickinson College. In order to address these issues, we decided to engage young people in collecting oral histories. We wanted to empower the students and foster academic work that spoke to their concerns. We also wanted to gain greater understanding of Carlisle's African Americans and to record and make available the rich history of a community that had not been included in the town's official history.

There were legitimate worries about continuing racial tensions and lack of integration in the town of Carlisle and about the potential repercussions of speaking out and appearing to be, as several narrators put it, "uppity." Oral history methodology provided a relatively safe, nonpoliticized way to collect information in this politically sensitive situation. The KKK still made its presence felt in the area, periodically placing fliers in rural mailboxes. In the initial study in 1989–90 we used pseudonyms for all narrators, since a number felt uncomfortable speaking out, knowing that they could be identified.

By 2001, when we began the second stage of the project, the climate in the town had shifted somewhat. An interracial Social Justice Committee was active. When the KKK threatened to march, many organizations and churches came together to organize a large unity rally, with support from the governor of Pennsylvania and the Pennsylvania Human Rights Commission, as a counter to what turned out to be a very small KKK gathering. By then, most narrators wanted to use their own names when we interviewed them.

During the fall of 2001, two groups of students at Dickinson came together for the second stage, a follow-up study of Carlisle's African American community and race relations in town and on campus. This time the team of Dickinson students was much larger and more diverse than had been the case a decade earlier. One set of students was enrolled in a qualitative research methods class in sociology. The other set came from the Crossing Borders program, a cross-cultural (inter- and intracultural) program that brought together up to twenty students from Dickinson and two historically black universities in New Orleans, Xavier University of Louisiana and Dillard University. The students spent the summer in Cameroon, West Africa. They returned to Dickinson for the fall semester and then spent the spring semester at one of the historically black universities. During the fall all Crossing Borders participants took one course that focused on the African diaspora and on historical and contemporary race relations.

Wanting to discover more about the community of which Dickinson College is a part, and to enrich their study of race relations, these two groups of students were eager to engage in a study of Carlisle. Their focus was on the local African American community, which is rarely visited by students despite its nearness to the campus.

As they began their research at the local historical society in 2001, students became increasingly convinced of the project's importance. Compared to the documentation of Euro-Americans (mainly Scots-Irish and Germans) who had settled in the area, the information on African Americans in Carlisle was very limited. Most of the family genealogical records focused on prominent Euro-American families. The students, therefore, relied primarily on the oral history interviews done as part of the 1989–90 community-college collaboration, as well as on census data, city directories, and funeral directories. Using these various sources, they began to piece together the history of the African American community in Carlisle.

This history dates back to the 1700s. Some of the earliest African Americans were brought to the area as slaves to work on farms, in homes, and in the iron industry. Others came as free blacks to work in the iron mills—including the Pine Grove furnace—as unskilled laborers, and as domestic servants. Carlisle developed into a segregated black and white town, with few other racial or ethnic minorities. African Americans worked at unskilled or low-skilled jobs, and local businesses successfully kept out the unions. Throughout the twentieth century, only a few black professionals (doctors, dentists, ministers, and teachers) lived in the community. By the time we began our research in 1989, there were no black medical professionals and only two black teachers in the whole school district.

As the students listened to the previously recorded oral history interviews, they were captivated by the narrators' passion and humor in recounting their stories. They expressed both eagerness and fear as they imagined conducting their own interviews. Would they be able to effectively cross racial and class lines? For many of the students, the first step was to get beyond the timidity they felt about interviewing people who appeared to be different from them. This was particularly true for many of the white students, but it also was the case with students of color. These shared misgivings helped the students realize that their fear was often as much about taking the initiative to start a personal conversation as it was about race. Would people be willing to talk with them? What did they, as interviewers, have to offer?

They eased their way into the black community by going to church services and meeting people afterwards. Then they branched out. Many of the students chose to do follow-up interviews with narrators from the first stage of the project and their families. Others sought out new connections.

The First Stage: 1989–90

It wasn't a sweet life. No, I wouldn't call it a sweet life because you had a lot to contend with, you know. What was it like growing up in Carlisle? Bad! Just like putting a chicken in a bear's cave.
—Rachael Hodge, age 94

In 1989, two black high school students, Shelli and Richelle, sat around a table at Shiloh Baptist Church as a group of older people brainstormed plans for the college-community collaboration. Present were a black minister, a white high school teacher, a black elementary school teacher (the only African American teacher in the school district at the time), two white college professors, and two white college students. The "Carlisle Community Project: An Interracial Collaboration" would involve oral histories, videotaped documentaries, professional conference presentations, History Day workshops, and community publication of stories told and written by members of the black community. Uncertain and certainly overwhelmed, the two eleventh-graders glanced furtively at each other with looks that clearly communicated: "What did we get ourselves into, and how fast can we get out of here?"

Finally, the scholarly talk was put on hold. All discussion of oral history methodology, family histories, and community research was pushed into the cracks, like mortar between the cement blocks of the church basement. The tape player was cued up and the voice of Rachael Hodge, a ninety-four-year-old widow and community matriarch who lived across the street from the church, rang out. The high school students listened intently as Hodge told of growing up black in predominantly white Carlisle at the turn of the century.

> I was born in Carlisle in 1895, delivered by my grandmother in a house right down the street from here. I never knew my mother since she died giving me birth but my grandmother took care of me.
>
> What was it like growing up in Carlisle? Bad! . . .
>
> I went to school at the black school until eighth grade, and then I went to the high school that technically was integrated. But we got a different diploma.
>
> After high school, there wasn't anywheres for you to climb. There was nothing for you to do—what I mean no pick. You had to work, as they had used the expression, "in a white folks' kitchen." You had to be a cook or a waitress or a maid. Sometimes you could get a job nursing, you know, and that kept you out on the street pushing this baby up and down. You couldn't find much to do. No polished jobs. . . . I wouldn't call it a sweet life because you had a lot to contend with.
>
> You know, you—the white people—I hate to say this, but the white people caused a lot of trouble because you could be sitting at your own door, standing at your own door, not even botherin' them and they'd go holler "NIGGER!" and when they said "NIGGER" that meant "FIGHT!" That was all there was to it, and then, of course, they were never bothering you; it was always you bothering them. But our boys and girls just didn't take it off them. I know one thing, the white people couldn't have stood it. You'd have took low, [*pause*] yes, [*pause*] yes.

In this first interview, Mrs. Hodge was ready to "tell it like it is," acknowledging that she was speaking to white listeners: Marianne Esolen, a white (actually Italian American) college student, and me, a white college professor. Enough rapport and respect had been established that she felt comfortable sharing her story with us, interjecting at times: "You, you whites would have took low." It helped that Mrs. Hodge was ninety-four, old enough to care little (not to be confused with not caring at all) about what others thought. I also had my three-month-old son with me, which helped open up a conversation about birthing and babies.

> I know a woman that had a baby—a colored baby, and the white woman was admiring this baby and she said, "If you wasn't black, I'd kiss you!" Well, you never saw anything rub off us. We're this color and we can't help it.

Although Mrs. Hodge talked about times that stretched some eighty years into the past, she spoke with a vivid clarity and passion. As the tape played, the expressions on Shelli's and Richelle's faces changed from confusion and boredom to excitement and interest. To paraphrase oral historian Paul Thompson, as those of us gathered in that church basement listened to Rachael Hodge, she gave history back in her own words. She recognized the heroism of ordinary people going about their daily lives and gave voice to their experience. In that moment, Rachael Hodge brought history out of and into the Carlisle community, affecting everyone around that table in different yet powerfully similar ways.

For the two black high school students, Shelli and Richelle, the project provided an opportunity to explore their own family and community history and in so doing to rediscover their past, make sense of the present, and plan for the future. For Andi, a white high school English teacher, the project offered a way to empower her high school students by legitimizing work that was relevant to their lives and to explore longstanding questions of race and racism as they pertained to the Carlisle school system. For Jill and me, both white college professors, and Marianne, a white college student, the project offered an opportunity to become better integrated into the Carlisle community and to integrate teaching and research around important local issues. For everyone, the project became a lesson in self-examination, community awareness, and the challenges and rewards of ethnographic research, focusing on the collection of oral histories.

While we were all captivated by the rich, tremulous voice on the tape, Shelli and Richelle were particularly enthralled. They did not know Mrs. Hodge personally, but they knew her by reputation as one of the black "community mothers," and they knew she lived in a certain house they walked past every day. They were enchanted by the voice of a woman describing real experiences that were both radically different from and strikingly similar to their own. Growing up and attending high school in Carlisle, Shelli and Richelle saw every day what Mrs. Hodge had seen in her lifetime: members of their community who graduated from high school, only to stand on the corner or sit in the park or push their own babies up and down the street. Shelli and Richelle knew about being called "nigger," and they knew about having to fight. They knew kids hanging out on the street corner, but they also knew there was more to the community than that.

Mrs. Hodge's narrative probed issues, experiences, and feelings that weren't always considered polite topics of conversation. Both Shelli and Richelle seemed surprised and impressed by her candor as she openly discussed racism in Carlisle at the turn of the century. They also wondered what we, the committee of "older people," more than half of us white, were thinking and feeling as we listened to those same words.

Shelli, in particular, was ready to get involved. She wanted to interview and tell the stories of various young people, both those who didn't hang out on the street corners and those who did. She wanted to give them a chance to speak and she wanted to speak herself. Rachael Hodge did not just tell Shelli a story that was memorable in its hearing; she encouraged Shelli to speak out herself and to engage in a dialogue that went beyond the stereotypes of age and race. She encouraged Shelli to become both a researcher and a historian for her own generation and her own community.

Soon after that first church basement meeting, Shelli and Marianne began working together in a mutually beneficial partnership. Shelli had entrée and insight into the African American community. Marianne had training in oral history methodology, so she was able to help Shelli shape the questions she wanted to ask of her peers. Drawing on her own experience with discrimination in the local high school, Shelli chose as her first interview another black high school student named Pamela:

> I would say most white kids are scared of the black kids, but I would not know why. I mean think about it, 700 and some white kids [*laughs*] and maybe forty blacks.

As Pamela continues, she makes clear that she found not only the students but also the teachers to be afraid and prejudiced:

> They act like there's a lot of us. *They* watch *us*. I mean it's true, some of the black people do live up . . . to the stereotypes people give us, but most of us don't. We go to school and all of us like to socialize; you just don't want to go to class, walk, go to class, walk. . . . And it's just like you get tired of being called THOSE people. . . . If it was like 700 blacks and maybe 150 whites then I would see there was maybe a reason for them [teachers] to act the way they do towards blacks. . . . They act like blacks are a threat, and it's really sad because teachers are supposed to be there to help you, and they're supposed to want you to do more and they're there to encourage you to do more, but it doesn't seem that some of the teachers do that.
> SHELLI: It's amazing to me when a group of blacks will be standing somewhere and four, five, six times as many whites will be standing and they'll be scared of the blacks. I mean what put that fear? I don't understand why that fear is there.

As we continued to conduct interviews, it became clear that other African American students in Carlisle shared Shelli's understanding of black students' position vis-à-vis white students and the high school faculty and administration. Realizing that others were afraid of them gave them an inverted sense of power—the kind of power that does not empower but entraps. Pamela explained, "It's scary, 'cause when you're there and being black and seeing things from a black point of view, it really looks hopeless. . . . I know I probably will do what I want to do and be what I want to be, but some kids just don't have hope."

In 1991, both Shelli and Pamela planned to leave Carlisle after graduation, Pamela to go to college and Shelli to go to college or into the armed services. "If you want to be somebody, you have to leave Carlisle," Shelli explained. "You have to get out." Shelli expressed aspirations for her future children and for Carlisle, too.

> I never want my kids to have to go through being stereotyped . . . being judged before you're known, being called something that you're totally opposite from. I just want everybody to give my kids a chance. . . . Before you judge them, get to know them. Before you determine who they are and what they stand for, get to know them. . . . Don't ever assume something . . . you can't *assume* about people . . . I mean, you can assume it's gonna rain. You can't assume people. . . . That isn't possible because your assumptions when it comes to people are most all the time wrong. . . . I hope someday there is not a Carlisle black community, not a Carlisle white community, just the Carlisle community.

As we conducted interviews, listened to tapes, and read transcriptions during the project's first stage, we were working out our own understandings of what was going on in the community and also within ourselves. The project became a very personal one as we moved in and out of our roles as insider/outsider, historian/listener, participant/observer, minority/majority, student/teacher, apprentice/mentor.[3] Shelli's final journal entry reflects both the skepticism and the hope that characterized her involvement in the project and her relationship to Carlisle:

> When first approached about this project I was very reluctant. I couldn't understand why—why these people? I felt like this was just going to be another thing to help the "Poor Black Community," and like everything else nothing would be done to make a change. I feel we've made a change to some of the few people we've reached, including myself. Before I began, I never knew how deep and how long the problems have been here. Some of the problems Rachael Hodge faced eighty years ago, myself and Pamela still face today. For the people of my generation I think the biggest concern lies with the Carlisle School District. Before I started the project I had no idea how bad it was. . . . The most important thing I've realized as a result of the project is that I must make a change. Until someone speaks out, everything will stay the same forever.

Shelli's sentiments reveal the ways in which oral history "brings history into, and out of, the community," as Thompson says. "Oral history gives history back to the people in their own words. And in giving a past, it also helps them towards a future of their own making."[4]

For those of us who came to the project as observers looking to become participants, helping the community discover and document its stories allowed us to discover our own communities and stories as well. Marianne Esolen, a white sociology major, wrote about her awareness of her role as a researcher and her evolving self-consciousness in the conclusion to her honors thesis:

> When I began my research on Carlisle's black community it was not without some insecurity, apprehension, and confusion. I worried about my color, my age, my status as a [college] student, my religion, my gender . . . in short I wondered where I would fit into this community as a student researcher. I wondered who would respond to me and how they would respond. I wondered how I would approach my interviews and how my approach would be interpreted. I wondered if I would step on toes while addressing sensitive issues. Later I wondered if others worried about stepping on my toes while addressing sensitive issues. I wondered how any of this would get started and where any of it would go. I wondered if I would ever feel less the outsider and I wondered if I would gain the trust and rapport necessary to do justice to the research of Carlisle's black community. Basically I wondered and worried and wondered. . . .
>
> I was quite often embarrassed and sometimes even frightened by my race. I felt guilty, disgusted, and angry when hearing of various racial incidents. My skin color for the first time in my life was something I felt shame for, an interesting role-reversal given the focus of this research. I no longer so easily made the distinction between THEM—the racist whites who committed any number of crimes against humanity—and US, the liberal post–civil rights movement generation of whites who so quickly, so completely, and so assuredly made the declaration of our independence from the weight of their prejudice and the guilt of choices, attitudes, and excuses based on those prejudices.
>
> For an olive-skinned Italian who grew up in an all-white community and only heard the racial slur "nigger" used in reference to myself as an Italian, this sudden confusion over my own racial "pride and prejudice" left me unprepared for my objective outsider role as researcher. I found myself walking on eggshells I already imagined to exist whether they were actually a reality or not. As a result of this super-self-consciousness, my confidence was at least in part left in my car as I walked up to the door of those first participants, nervously took too many notes, and stumbled through the technical difficulties of dead batteries, forgotten tapes, and inkless pens.

Ironically this period of introspection and self-doubt I believe was the most fruitful contributor to my development as a researcher. As I shed many of my own misconceptions about myself, issues of racism, and one's responsibility to address such issues, I became empowered by my research, its purpose, value, and absolute necessity. I knew I was still white, but I also knew I was committed, and I believe this commitment to the project and to the people within Carlisle's community surpassed many of the racial barriers initially present in my first set of interviews. I was no longer defensive because I no longer felt so self-conscious. I became the researcher and "listener" and members of the community became participants and "historians." The relationships that ensued were by and large based on trust, respect, and surprise—the subtle wonder that a white college student was collecting black family histories and that members of that community were allowing her to do so.

The Second Stage: 2001

A decade later, the diverse team of students from Dickinson, Dillard, and Xavier universities built upon and expanded the work we had done in the first stage of the project. For Aja, an African American student from Xavier participating in the Crossing Borders program, the work in Carlisle's black community was the highlight of her experience at Dickinson. Originally from St. Louis, Aja felt very comfortable going into the community and stopping to talk with people sitting on the sidewalks or on park benches. She soon found in Mr. Conn, an octogenarian and former housekeeper for a Dickinson fraternity for many decades, "the grandfather I never had." She was invited to birthday parties and Sunday dinners at his home. Val, an African American student from the Bronx, had a totally different experience. She felt quite uncomfortable going into the community and talking with people. She had as much anxiety as many of the white students did about how people would view her and about whether or not they would be willing to talk with her. This became an interesting part of the class conversation as it became clear that race was not the only, or perhaps even the most salient, issue for everyone. A host of other considerations came into play: personality, regional and urban/rural background, and socioeconomic class.

Many members of the African American community in Carlisle mentioned feeling more comfortable with students of color from the South. Used to the warmth of Southern hospitality, these students often could more easily approach people and start conversations in a friendly and respectful way. The majority of Carlisle's black families originally came from the

South, some of them generations ago. Some members of the community perceived the Northern-raised students of color, who were predominantly from urban areas, to be less friendly, less respectful, and more arrogant. "The ones from the North, from the city, they just walk by and don't say anything; they don't even see us." When Val heard this, she said, "Well, yeah, you are taught not to look people in the eye in the city. You've got to be crazy to do that, to trust people." At the end of the semester, Val commented, "Reflecting on how it's changed me . . . I'm thinking about who I was before. You know, I knew everything. 'If you're black, this is how you act, if you're white, this is how you act.' Of course there's a few exceptions to the rules, but you know, basically this is how we are. *How we is.*"

These insights and conversations—about what it meant to be black, to be raced as white, to be biracial and feel as though one had to choose or not—became more complex and nuanced as we moved through the semester. Having a diverse group of students and faculty involved definitely benefited our explorations of race and race relations, of our own and others' identities, and of other people's perceptions of us. As a group, we were able to consider more fully the ways in which race influences expectations and interactions and the ways in which other factors and experiences contribute as well. Such discussions proved to be both confusing and liberating.

The oral history research drew on the resources of all of us, students and teachers alike. It challenged us to step out of our traditional roles as educators and students and explore social interactions that were both part of the history we were documenting and part of the present we were living. It forced us to think about ourselves in relation to others.

As we discover and tell other people's stories, we need to hear both what they are telling us and what we are telling ourselves. In "Oral History as Ethnographic Encounter," Micaela di Leonardo concludes that the new work in ethnographic theory offers oral history two major contributions: "the self-conscious analysis of the intersubjectivity of the interview, and an admission of the innately theoretical nature of any interview project."[5]

In confronting issues of methodology and interpretation in a collaborative project like this one, we cannot escape the complex and difficult issues that surface as part of the research process. As Thompson reminds us, "All history depends ultimately upon its social purpose."[6] We continually had to confront this fact as we went about our work, negotiating what questions we should ask, whom we should interview next, which materials and findings we should present and to whom. As we worked on our interpretations of the data that reflected who we were and what roles we played, it became clear that important methodological questions posed sensitive personal and political questions.

The relationship between the project and the larger community was an interactive one, representing a "series of exchanges, a dialectic, between information and interpretation," between educators and students and their localities, and between races, classes, and generations.[7] When approached about their willingness to be interviewed, most of the adult narrators initially responded, "I haven't anything to say." We interpreted this as having at least two possible meanings: one, they didn't want to talk to us, and/or two, they didn't believe they had much to say that was worthy of being recorded. We assured each potential narrator that his or her story was important and noted that other community members had been willing to share their stories; everyone we approached ultimately agreed to an interview. Their positive responses were partly due to the fact that the high school students, who came from their own community, as well as the college students, seemed genuinely interested in listening to them. And for many of the narrators, the interviews provided an opportunity to instruct a younger generation, as though they were talking to their own grandchildren. As for the younger narrators, they were just waiting for a chance to speak and to be heard, and it was by and large their peers who were interviewing them.

Discovering and Recovering Relationality

> As we discover, we remember; remembering, we discover; and most intensely do we experience this when our separate journeys converge.
> —Eudora Welty, *One Writer's Beginnings*

> Exploring difference is about relationship. It is about bringing ourselves, again and again, to the edge of our not knowing, to the edge of our silences, to the edge of subjects that feel, and sometimes are, dangerous. Each time, we play out the drama of difference: when we reach that edge, when we come up to a moment of pain or confusion or impasse, what do we do? Do we stay or do we leave, do we continue to speak in the presence of these feelings or do we close down around them and retreat to the world we know? To hold difference and sustain hope requires us, moment by moment, to hold steady, to stay with ourselves and each other, to continue to learn how to speak in the presence of profound silences.
> —Jill McLean Taylor, Carol Gilligan, and Amy M. Sullivan, *Between Voice and Silence: Women and Girls, Race and Relationship*

As students conducted, transcribed, and shared their interviews, they were processing not only information but also their own and others' emotional responses to that information. At various times they were shocked, surprised, angered, relieved, or awed by what they heard *and experienced* as they interviewed people. The process of interviewing is one of mutual engagement, and the students were drawn into the lives of their narrators. As they came to know these neighbors whom they had never before visited, they were challenged to think not only about the past but also about the present and about what the future might hold. They soon realized that this study was not just about "the other" but also about themselves, their assumptions, and their relationships.

This became clear when Dickinson College students Jesse Morrell and Jesse Shellock interviewed Jack Hodge, a seventy-six-year-old man who worked as a cafeteria monitor at Carlisle High School. About two-thirds of the way through the interview, Mr. Hodge spoke about discrimination and racism and the ways in which some things were changing:

> So we're on the move. Slow, we're not as far as should be . . . but we're coming. And look, prejudice is always gonna be around, let's face it. You know? You are going to have those who don't like you because the way you comb your hair, or the way you look or something. . . . But I let it be their problem. What you see with me is what you get and I can't control this, you know? I am what I am, but I can be a good person, you know? And you got some white people too who, you know, are the same way. . . . I know who I am, what I am. . . . I would never do you any harm, that's not what life is all about. I always believe in sitting down, get to know me. Get to talk to me. Get to know me, and then you find out.

Mr. Hodge related a story from work:

> I used to work in Camp Hill. . . . And there was a lady down there [named Buela], and she was a Mennonite and I noticed that when I walked down the aisle there in the store, she would sorta cringe and move away from me, you know? Wouldn't touch me, you know? I thought okay, so, I can be a devil at times. . . . Sometimes I would just rub her, hit her, with the elbow. Boy did she jump! So one day, I was working on my press, and I burnt my arm. Just took the top of the skin off. So I went over and I said, "Buela, where is that there cream at?" And she said, "What did you do?" And I said, "I burnt myself!" And she said, "Okay," and she got the cream and she said, "Let's see it," and I showed her. "Oh, you're white, you're white!" And I said, "What in the hell do you think I am?" She thought that I was black all through, I swear to God. To this day, we are good friends.

JESSE S.: Really?

MR. HODGE: Yes, because she got to know me. She had never worked around black people before, you know. . . . But Carlisle is—it has changed, and it is changing. It's still a lot of prejudice here and always will be. It's not [so much] out in the open the way it used to be, it's sorta underneath, subdued now, yeah.

The reference point for this comparison was the more overt racism that Mr. Hodge had experienced as a little boy:

I remember when I was a little guy, *and you're gonna love this*. The freshmen at Dickinson College—

JESSE S.: Oh no!

MR. HODGE: Yeah . . .

This is as good an illustration of the dialogic nature of the interview as I can imagine. Here, Mr. Hodge recognizes that the students are listeners who are involved in the process of his storytelling. He emphasizes, *"you're gonna love this."* He seems to know intuitively, as oral historian Alessandro Portelli puts it, that the *"inter-*view" involves a "mutual sighting."[8] It is about the engagement between the narrator and the listener, both of whom are *seen, heard,* and *affected.*

Mr. Hodge went on to recall what happened in 1936, when he was ten or eleven years old:

The Dickinson students—the freshman—wore white pants, white shirts, little red bow ties, and red blazers, and red caps, you know? That was the freshmen dress. . . . When they were pledging, they would have to come out and grab a little black boy and they had these big paddles, great big paddles. And they would grab and whip him, beat him.

JESSE S.: Are you serious?

MR. HODGE: Yeah, I'm serious! Yeah.

JESSE S.: What were they pledging?

MR. HODGE: I don't know, whatever fraternity it was up there. . . . So, there was a lady there, we were all sittin' on the porch here because we weren't allowed to come uptown after dinner, we just didn't, because, um, you got into trouble and your parents worried about you, so you sit there on the steps. And she heard us talking about these students coming out and grabbing us and whipping us, you know? So she said what you have to do is set on down on the curb and make some nice, wet mud balls . . . don't make 'em tight or hard, you don't want to hurt anybody. But make 'em nice and wet and muddy, you know. And then when they come after the kid to paddle him, then throw these mud balls at them. So one time, we knew they were coming around—they would circle the block, you know—and one of the kids would sit there and we would be hiding behind these bushes and everything you know. And about three or four of 'em would jump out of the car and come over and grab him. And we were waiting until they got close, and when they got close, we let them have these mud balls. Oh man, I'm tellin' you, you have never seen anything like that, I mean they ran. They had on the white pants, the white shirts, you know? And we just let them have these fat, juicy, wet mud balls. Boy, they dropped the paddles, some went runnin' to get back into the car, some just ran up the street back towards the college. And that, that's how we broke that up, really.

JESSE S.: So they stopped doing that after that?

MR. HODGE: Yeah, yeah.

JESSE S.: Good!

MR. HODGE: Ah sure!

JESSE S.: Good job!

In reporting on the interview later to the class, Jesse and Jesse shared excerpts from the written transcripts and the videotape. They commented on the substance of the interview and their desire to get more information about the Dickinson freshmen of that time. The most poignant moment came, however, when they were asked how they *felt* during that part of the interview. Jesse Shellock responded, "Well, I was shocked. I couldn't believe it." She then went on quickly to play more of the tape in which she circled back to the mud ball story after about four minutes of conversation about other subjects, including a discussion of racism at the Army War College.

JESSE S.: Did any of your friends—it didn't happen to you—that fraternity paddle thing?

MR. HODGE: No, they didn't get me.

JESSE S.: Okay. Did any of your really close friends, have it happen to?

MR. HODGE: Oh yeah! My buddies, my buddies got paddled.

JESSE S.: Really?

MR. HODGE: Heck yeah!

JESSE S.: Did their parents try to do anything?

MR. HODGE: What are you gonna do?

JESSE S.: Did their parents try to notify the police?

MR. HODGE: Oh, oh the police.

JESSE S.: [*laughs*] No? Bad idea?

MR. HODGE: Oh, come on! The police, the police, where were the police you know?

JESSE S.: So they didn't care, that little kids that were ten were getting the crap kicked out of them?

MR. HODGE: That's right, right. They would just say, well just sit in front of your—don't go out of the neighborhood, just sit in front of your door. And back in them days it was really something; sure, no kidding.

JESSE S.: Wow.

MR. HODGE: Sure, no kidding. We remember, I remember when we see the police coming, we'd run. We didn't do anything. But we ran. They don't run today, if you notice, they don't run today. But hey, God's been good to us and helped us to grow and learn and get to know people and talk to people. What else is there in life? You know. That you look back on it and say, hey man, you missed something, in not being able to talk to me, for not taking the time out to find out who I am; that I'm okay. Yeah, hey, that guy's not bad just because he's black, you know. What the heck!

In that class discussion we talked about the relationships between college students and members of the African American community, now as well as then. This brought up questions related to race relations on campus. What assumptions did students of color and white students hold, what experiences did they have on campus, what it was like being white or being black at Dickinson? It also brought up differences between individual students of color and their different relationships with members of the African American community. The discovery that some townspeople felt more comfortable with the African American students from the South opened up questions about regional differences and similarities, about class and gender, and about differences between urban, rural, and small-town cultures. Recognizing and analyzing these differences helped students both to *see* race and to see beyond it—to the complex interactions that race has with class, gender, sexual orientation, age, region, and religion.

Most important, students learned to ask and to listen—both to the people who were willing to share their stories and to themselves. They thought about how they were feeling as they heard stories of discrimination, and they came to understand that discrimination is intensely personal and can leave scars. The African American narrators, recalling their childhoods, emphasized that race affected everything: where you could go, where you could sit in a movie theater, where you could eat or swim. As Marcus Hodge, the son of Rachael Hodge, recounted:

Well, where the dam is . . . that was specifically reserved for the whites. And the blacks used to have to go down by the pump house and swim. . . . That's the truth. All the whites would go up to the dam, and all the blacks, the Afro-Americans, they would go by the pump house and swim. Now we'd fish all over the place. Allowed to fish anywhere we wanted to [and ice skate] anywhere we wanted to. But, as far as swimming goes, no, we couldn't go up there and contaminate that water up there.

Robert Owens, the first (and so far only) African American to be elected to the Carlisle Borough Council, recollected:

> If you went to the movies you had to sit a certain place in the theater. You had to sit up in the balcony, way in the back. You could not sit on the main floor of the theaters. Tickets were the same price, but you weren't allowed to go anywhere else in the theater. We couldn't even belong to the YMCA. And that change was made less than thirty years ago [in the late 1960s]. . . . So it hasn't been long that we could belong to the YMCA, or the Lions, or the Kiwanis . . . there was no thought of such things in the thirties, forties, or fifties. The other big thing was housing. . . . We built this house in 1967, and it almost took me an act of Congress to get the money for this house. Just to give you an example, at that time I was working and I had a good job, a very good job. My wife was working and had a good job. Our joint income was up in the upper-middle-class level at the time when I went to get a loan for this house. We had already owned two houses, we didn't owe anybody anything; I mean, our cars were paid for and everything was fine with my salary, but the bank would not give me the money to start. No reason at all; just because of who I was.

Although a number of narrators said they had put these experiences behind them, their words, voices, and faces suggested otherwise, that thirty, sixty, and even eighty years later they remembered these injustices. As one narrator in his seventies reflected,

> Some of these things, I am not bitter about these, but some of these things still bother me. I think of how long it has gone on, and there's still an awful lot of it in Carlisle. It's more covert now, but there's still an awful lot [of prejudice and discrimination].

Reflexive Analysis and Authenticity

For some students, stories of racist discrimination brought up painful memories; for other students, they brought up feelings of guilt. We listened to expressions of both emotions, and in the process we came to know one another much more deeply. Knowing that guilt can paralyze rather than politicize, we talked about guilt, shame, anger, blame, and responsibility—and about how to move beyond guilt to action. We became increasingly aware of how much the history and institutionalization of slavery and racism affect all of us and sensitive to the particular forms that racism assumes in the United States (as contrasted to, for example, the Caribbean or Brazil). The writings of Michel-Rolph Trouillot and

Avery Gordon, and their images of the ghost, were particularly useful in deepening our analysis.

> That U.S. slavery has officially ended, yet continues in many complex forms—most notably institutionalized racism and the cultural denigration of blackness—makes its representation particularly burdensome in the United States. Slavery here is a ghost, both the past and a living presence.[9]

As we moved through the semester, it became increasingly clear that, as Trouillot argues, "what needs to be denounced here to restore authenticity is much less slavery than the racist present within which representations of slavery are produced. . . . Authenticity implies a relation with what is known that duplicates the two sides of historicity: it engages us both as actors and narrators"—and as students and teachers. "Whether it invokes, claims, or rejects The Past, authenticity obtains only in regard to current practices that engage us as witnesses, actors, and commentators. . . . Even in relation to The Past our authenticity resides in the struggles of our present."[10] Shelli certainly understood this. When Marianne first asked her how she would describe the general relationship between the white community and the black community in Carlisle, she immediately responded:

> I think it's fake. Like there's this fake front that everything's perfect and everything's all nice, neat, tied up in a little bow, you know: the whites are trying to help the blacks, and the blacks are trying to help the whites and vice versa. And there's a great cultural exchange when actually there's not, because, just look. I mean, all's you got to do is *observe* things. I mean there's not many blacks in Carlisle, and the ones that are in Carlisle are isolated from a lot of whites, I mean, there's no blacks holding positions. . . . I don't think there's any blacks on the school board or anything like that. I know there's a black running for borough council . . . very few black teachers. There's no learning about black people, black history. There's no education about blacks to white students or blacks to black students for that matter. [*voice raised*] I mean, black students are just as ignorant about their culture as white students are ignorant about black culture. Because they were never taught.

As we discussed the ways in which historical memory is contested and becomes a site of cultural struggle, we examined how dominant and alternative historical narratives have affected our own lives and understandings as well as those of our narrators. We began to deal with contested truths, not only at the macro level, within the academic literature "out there," but also at the micro level, within the group and within ourselves. It was at this personal level, of course, that it became particularly difficult to explore the contested terrains that separated as well as united us.

The students came up against this as they discussed what they had learned and not learned about American history, about power, and about social constructions of race and ethnicity across time and place. They struggled with this as they explored the meaning of the accusation sometimes hurled by blacks against one another: "You're acting white." For most of the white students, whiteness was only just beginning to become visible. They were trying to figure out what it meant to be white, while most of the African American students were working at another level to deconstruct what it meant. We explored what blackness and whiteness meant both politically and personally and how students believed they could or should express themselves on a predominantly white campus.

For Serena, an African American student from Xavier University, the experiences she had while working on the project allowed her to interact more comfortably with both her black and white friends, without always having to code-switch and self-censor:

> I no longer trip. . . . Some of my black friends were in my face, "Why are you talking to white people?" Now I'm not tripping—now I don't care what anyone thinks about who I'm walking with. I used to have a certain lingo with my black friends, and one with my white friends, and now—it's all the same now, more universal. I mean, we are applying what we've been learning to our lives right now.

As Trouillot argues, "any historical narrative is a particular bundle of silences, the result of a unique process, and the operation required to deconstruct these silences will vary accordingly."[11] So is it too with personal and group narratives. In fact, this particular group had a remarkable and respectful way of calling one another out, holding one another accountable in ways that enabled us to move beyond defensiveness.

Remembering, Discovering, Reconciling

> *Recordar:* To remember; from the Latin re-cordis, to pass back through the heart.
> —Eduardo Galeano

This account of collecting and analyzing oral histories in an African American community in small-town America tells us much about the wider community and its subgroups, and about those who are interacting with and doing research in the community. Community studies is not just about examining demographic and economic data and specific historical events, though these are critical to understanding historical and social context. To understand community, we must also understand the dynamics of relationships, especially relationships between dominant and subordinate groups and between community members who have more power, influence, and resources (material, educational, occupational) and those who have less. We must investigate how power and influence are defined and negotiated, and we must look into the heart and soul of communities, as well as their social, political, and economic conditions.

Students came to appreciate and respect the people whom they interviewed, recognizing what the narrators had achieved and the obstacles they had overcome to do so. The students, in the words of oral historian Paul Thompson, came to value the extraordinary lives of seemingly ordinary people.[12] This is not something I taught my students; it is something they learned *in relating* to those with whom they talked and worked. Most students were initially fearful about asking sensitive questions of others and hearing their responses, but this fear soon gave way to excitement and ultimately to a sense of reward. Perhaps most surprising to the students was people's willingness to tell their stories—painful stories of discrimination and loss, as well as stories of accomplishment and perseverance—if they, the listeners, showed genuine interest. This authentic connection and generosity of spirit made the experience a rich and meaningful one.

Hearing the stories also helped students see more clearly the dynamics of campus relationships. They began to think concretely about to how to make Dickinson a more welcoming place for everyone, and they started doing just that through their own actions and relationships. Oral history projects are not just a history of "the other"; they are an inquiry into our relationships with one another. They are an exploration of the past and present of all of us, revealing the ways in which race, religion, class, gender, sexuality, age, religion, and other differences and similarities are negotiated. This then is the challenge: to understand the past in all its complexity, both what happened and what is said to have happened; to understand the present and how it is perceived; and to imagine and shape the future.

Notes

1. ALANA is increasingly being used within higher education, especially in admissions, to refer to African America, Latina/o, Asian, and Native American people, replacing the terms *minority* or *underrepresented*.

2. Median household income for African Americans in Carlisle was $26,250, with a per capita income of $12,748. In the black population twenty-five years of age and older, 74 percent have graduated from high school and 12 percent have a bachelor's degree or higher. Three-quarters of African Americans in the borough rent their homes (all figures from the 2000 census).

3. The project adopted the terminology used by Audrey Olsen Faulkner in her collection of the life histories of elderly African Americans in Newark, New Jersey. Faulkner referred to herself and other researchers as "listeners," while those being interviewed, the informants, were "historians." This terminology recognizes the narrators as the experts in telling and interpreting their own life stories. Faulkner, *When I Was Comin' Up: An Oral History of Aged Blacks* (Hamden, CT: Shoe String Press, 1982).

4. Paul Thompson, *The Voice of the Past: Oral History* (New York: Oxford University Press, 1988), 23, 308.

5. Micaela di Leonardo, "Oral History as Ethnographic Encounter," *Oral History Review* 15 (Spring 1987): 20.

6. Thompson, *Voice of the Past*, 1.

7. Ibid., 23.

8. Alessandro Portelli, *The Death of Luigi Trastulli and Other Stories: Form and Meaning of Oral History* (Albany: SUNY Press, 1990), 31.

9. Michel-Rolph Trouillot, *Silencing the Past: Power and the Production of History* (Boston: Beacon Press, 1995), 147; see also Avery F. Gordon, *Ghostly Matters: Haunting and the Sociological Imagination* (Minneapolis: University of Minnesota Press, 1997).

10. Trouillot, *Silencing the Past*, 147, 150–51.

11. Ibid., 27.

12. Thompson, *Voice of the Past*.

Doing Oral Histories in the Shadow of 9/11

Fear, Secrecy, and Intimidation as Factors in Research

Irum Shiekh

> THE COURT: There is something you wanted to talk about up here?
> PROSPECTIVE JUROR: Yes.
> THE COURT: Come on up [to the side bar].
> THE COURT: Yes, ma'am.
> PROSPECTIVE JUROR: I am a Muslim. I am a Muslim. I don't want to do a jury.
> THE COURT: You don't want to participate? I can't understand you. You don't want to do what?
> PROSPECTIVE JUROR: I am a Muslim too, and so I don't want to take part in juror.
> THE COURT: You think you might not be fair in this case?
> PROSPECTIVE JUROR: I don't want to, you know, take the part. I don't want to take the part in juror. That's the way.
> THE COURT: Do you have some difficulty understanding or expressing yourself in English?
> PROSPECTIVE JUROR: Little bit.
> THE COURT: Okay . . . I am going to excuse you. Thanks.

This dialogue took place during the trial of Wael Kishk in Brooklyn, New York, in January 2002.[1] Wael, a twenty-one-year-old man from Egypt with a valid student visa, was detained on September 19, 2001, at New York's JFK airport after federal agents deemed him suspicious. Months later he was found guilty of lying to federal agents about his educational plans. Wael underwent a jury trial and two Muslims were included in the jury selection process.[2] One clearly stated that his English skills were imperfect and the court excused him. The second, whose words are transcribed above, expressed her fear to the judge on record and declined to participate in the trial.

I never met the prospective juror and I will never know why she chose to decline rather than participate and ensure that Wael would receive a fair trial. Her conversation with the judge has multiple readings. She might have been concerned about the other jurors' perceptions of her; perhaps they wouldn't trust her judgment and would accuse her of bias if she tried to explain the defendant's perspectives. Maybe she feared her participation would subject her to surveillance by intelligence officers or police. Maybe she trusted the government and assumed that Wael must have done something wrong to have been arrested. There are many unknowns in this dialogue, and there could be other fears that one cannot detect.

Each time I reread this dialogue, a chill runs through me. The prospective juror speaks volumes when she repeats, "I am a Muslim, I am a Muslim. I don't want to do a jury." Unfortunately, her fear is not an exception.

From 2002 to 2004, I carried out research for a PhD dissertation on the arrests, detentions, and deportations of individuals following the September 11, 2001, attacks. Approximately forty people shared their stories with me. They were largely representative of the population that was targeted in the post-9/11 sweeps: all were originally from countries in the Middle East or South Asia, and almost all were Muslim. Some were still being held in U.S. detention centers when I interviewed them. Others had been released within the United States and I met them in cities like New York. The great majority, however, had been deported to other countries on their release, and I met them in Egypt, Pakistan, Palestine, and India. I stayed in touch with my subjects for several years after completion of my dissertation to carry out additional research for a book and documentary.[3] With each new encounter, the subjects revealed new information and I gained new insights.

During my research I came to understand the many fears experienced by the former detainees and their friends and families. In particular, former detainees feared that sharing their stories could lead to additional harassment from government agents or difficulties in processing their pending immigration or citizenship cases.[4] Although I was usually able to establish trust over time, some remained hesitant. Others never stopped believing I was a spy working for the government. Distant family members and friends sometimes dissociated themselves from detainees for their own survival. In some situations, lawyers told their clients not to talk with others under investigation.

I also experienced fear myself, which was rooted in my identity as a Pakistani Muslim. Because of my religious and ethnic background, I felt that I could be a target of racial profiling and even placed behind bars for my academic research. It has always been dangerous to take a critical stance toward U.S. government policies when the nation is at war abroad and simultaneously searching for "enemies" within. This danger is compounded when the researcher is a member of the community under attack.

Changing Climate after 9/11

These anxieties were relatively new for me, although I have long been involved in political advocacy. Between 1999 and 2001 I did fieldwork for a documentary on the internment of Japanese Latin Americans in U.S. detention camps during World War II.[5] During this research, we found hundreds of photos, motion pictures, and written documents, especially in the U.S. National Archives, that described the operation to transport Japanese captives from Peru and several other Latin American countries to various parts of the United States and confine them in Department of Justice camps. The state of California provided funding for the documentary, and librarians, archivists, and community leaders were eager to support our research. We felt the outpouring of support as we collected photographs, home videos, testimonies, and documents. My own ethnicity was not in question, and even though I had a political agenda—demanding equal reparations and formal apology for Japanese Latin Americans—people generally perceived me as an objective researcher engaged in the production of scholarship.

The primary subject of the documentary was Art Shibayama, a seventy-year-old man from San Jose, California. He had been fighting a legal battle to demand reparations and an apology from the U.S. government. Both were denied to Japanese Latin Americans because they were not U.S. citizens or residents at the time of internment, unlike Japanese Americans. As late as the 1990s, internment was considered a taboo subject in American history. Although the 1988 Civil Liberties Act confirmed that the World War II internment was a shameful period in the nation's history, the Supreme Court refused to hear Art's claim. Determined to continue the fight, Art filed his case with the Inter-American Commission on Human Rights, an organ of the Organization of American States. He commented, "Government is a big machine. It is very hard to fight with it." I didn't really understand the significance of this statement at the time.

The 9/11 attacks caused a profound shift in the political atmosphere and in my personal outlook. On September 11, 2001, I was returning to the United States from Durban, South Africa, after attending the World Conference against Racism. The flight was grounded in Johannesburg as all flights into the United States were canceled. I spent the next three days in a hotel, watching tragic images of the burning towers and feeling sad for the death of thousands, my head full of unknown fears. Like most other Muslims, I fervently hoped that Muslims were not involved in this attack.

Three days after my return to the United States I started to hear about the arrests and detentions of additional "terrorist suspects" who looked very much like my family and me. We felt the sting of belonging to a stigmatized group. Reports of hate crimes also started to trickle in. The death of a forty-nine-year-old Indian Sikh, Balbir Singh Sodhi, on September 15, 2001, in Mesa, Arizona, sent a chilling message to all Muslim and Muslim-looking communities.[6]

My brother Anjum was subjected to government interrogation and investigation, even though he had served in the U.S. military for over twenty-five years and was a retired major-colonel. Anjum was not arrested, but his ordeal did not end with the search. Before 9/11, he had frequently flown his private plane without experiencing any trouble with airport security officers. But after 9/11, law enforcement officers routinely stopped him each time he arrived at the airport. Someone would notice his "Muslim looks" or "Muslim accent" and called the authorities to "feel safe." Disgusted by the racial profiling, Anjum ended up selling his plane.[7]

An FBI agent also questioned my younger brother, Shoib, in his office for four to five hours. She solicited his opinions on the 9/11 attacks and scrutinized his responses. His telephone lines were tapped for months; for all we know, he could still be under surveillance.

We endured a barrage of strange questions, comments, and jokes from the general public that connected us to terrorism. Children could be particularly blunt. A young African American child in an elementary school in Fremont, California, said to my sister Arfa, a volunteer tutor, "Muslims blew up the twin towers in New York. . . . When are you going to blow up this school?" A young white child at the Phoenix, Arizona, airport pointed to my twenty-three-year-old nephew Abdul and loudly asked his mother, "Do the terrorists look like him?" The mother neither corrected the child nor apologized to Abdul. Everyone standing in the queue became tense, and Abdul felt that all eyes were on him. Later, no one sat next to him on the Southwest flight, even though it was nearly full. Abdul felt embarrassed and insulted.

All of us have experienced innumerable "random" searches at airports. My sister-in-law Amala, who frequently travels abroad, wrote that each time she traveled, airport security interrogated her. At our family dinners we relate our most recent horrible airport experiences. Occasionally, when family friends with Muslim names or Muslim appearance join us, we realize that their experiences are not that different from our own. The more a person looks or sounds Muslim, the worse the treatment.

Before 9/11, as people of color living in the United States, we had experienced racial profiling and hate crimes. The recurrence, intensity, and severity of such incidents and the linking of every vulnerable Muslim-looking person to terrorism impelled me to systematically examine the patterns of detentions and deportations after 9/11.[8] As I did so, the constant awareness that people might see in me the face of an enemy affected all aspects of my research. I felt a sense of fear and hesitation when I visited detention centers, asked for court files, or examined the trial transcripts of former detainees. I was careful to dress as an educated professional who had come to visit the inmate for professional reasons. At the court office's reception desk, I gave the receptionist the reference number of the file, instead of the detainee's name, to obscure the inmate's identity. I reviewed the files in a private area of the office so as not to advertise the fact that I was looking at the legal files of once-suspected terrorists.

State Restrictions and Secrecy

One of the biggest obstacles to my research was the state's secrecy and restrictions around the topic of 9/11 detainees. Government officials did not return my multiple messages, declined to talk to me when they answered the phone by accident, constantly referred me to public relations officers, or asked me to write a proposal about my research and then never responded.

In some situations, when I finally did meet FBI officers or other government officials, they were guarded, terse, and defensive. They constantly defended the government's decision to detain undocumented immigrants and cited laws that technically justified the detentions. The response that came closest to an admission of wrongdoing was that it was an emergency situation and some people suffered. However, the officials did not find enforcement policies to be arbitrary, discriminatory, or abusive, either in general or after 9/11 in particular.

My first experience of government resistance came with a call I made to the San Francisco immigration office about a detainee housed in the Yuba County Jail in Marysville, California, in the summer of 2002. Through my work with the National Lawyers Guild, I learned about Saleem (a pseudonym), a young Afghani man from the San Francisco Bay Area. Even though his arrest for an immigration violation came before 9/11, after the attacks he was automatically placed in a special category of detainees because of his Muslim background. Therefore we needed special permission from the San Francisco office to visit him in Marysville. The immigration officer scolded me in a shrill voice for reminding her of a letter that I had written to her two weeks earlier, asking about the possibility of meeting Saleem. After she hung up, I was left with three choices: I could stop my research, wait for her promised response, or find creative ways to meet unofficially with the detainee in jail.

I chose the third. A few weeks later, with the help of his family members, I met Saleem during the jail's visiting hours. The young man was eager to return home to his mother and brother. He also asked me to send him some novels to read. Even though his arrest had concerned only immigration matters, after 9/11 FBI agents questioned him about his links to terrorism. He also informed me that a few other immigration detainees at the detention center were under investigation for terrorism. It has been over eight years since I met Saleem, and I still have not received any formal response from the San Francisco immigration office.

At the rest of the detention centers I visited, I made no effort to obtain official approval. Connections with family members, community organizers, and lawyers were sufficient to arrange visits to detainees.

The official process remains restrictive and secretive, even though a majority of the detainees have been released and deported. In 2008 I was working on a documentary about the Metropolitan Detention Center (MDC) in Brooklyn, New York, which housed many of the detainees whom I had interviewed. I heard that some outsiders had managed to visit the Special Housing Unit on the ninth floor, so I tried to arrange a visit myself by going through official channels. I researched the visitation policy for academic researchers and sent several e-mails. Someone finally responded and asked me to write a request or proposal stating why it was important for my research to visit the ninth floor of the MDC. I followed these instructions, and after a few months the public information officer at the MDC, Michael Truman, sent an e-mail stating, "We are not interested in participating in your research project." I inquired about an appeal process. He responded, "The warden's decision is final."[9]

Thinking that the Freedom of Information Act (FOIA) might help me, in November 2007 I wrote to the Federal Bureau of Prisons and requested copies of surveillance video taken by cameras installed on the ninth floor of the MDC between October 2001 and August 2002.[10] By the time of my request, these videotapes had already been discussed in a 2003 report by the Office of the Inspector General in the U.S. Department of Justice, which used them to substantiate detainees' allegations of abuse.[11] In September 2008 I hired a lawyer to work with the Federal Bureau of Prisons to process my FOIA request, and the Bureau responded three months later. They officially refused to release the videotapes, arguing that they needed to protect the privacy of security officers and other officials shown on the tapes.[12] My lawyer wrote an appeal letter in which he cited specific recent legal cases and argued, "Recent case law is in favor of releasing videotapes documenting detainee treatment, notwithstanding the privacy interests of those depicted in the video."[13] This was in February 2009; we are still waiting for a response.

I was not the only one who experienced access issues. Many lawyers were unable to meet their clients who were being held incommunicado, and they testified on this point in congressional hearings. Al-Badr Al-Hazmi, a Saudi national, was detained in Texas by the Immigration and Naturalization Service on September 17, 2001, and released seven days later. His attorney, Gerald Goldstein, testified before the Senate Judiciary Committee that the immigration service did not let him talk to his client for five days, despite Al-Hazmi's numerous requests for counsel. During this period, Al-Hazmi was interrogated several times. Goldstein stated during his testimony, "Many of my colleagues who represent past or current detainees share my view that this veil of secrecy serves only to shield the government from criticism."[14]

Uzma Naheed, the wife of detainee Anser Mahmood, recalled how her husband volunteered to go with immigration authorities to discuss an expired visa after they came to the family's house in Bayonne, New Jersey, on October 3, 2001. Two years later, during an interview in Lahore, Pakistan, her eyes filled with tears as she recalled her despair when she could not locate her husband:

> The night of the arrest ended and I still hadn't heard from Anser. The chief investigator had told me that they would let my husband call me. I waited and kept thinking that the phone would ring any minute and I could not sleep. The morning came and still there was no phone call. I sent the kids to school and continued waiting for the phone to ring.

In the afternoon, I called the chief investigator and asked him about Anser's whereabouts. He wouldn't tell me anything.

Then the kids returned from school and started asking about their father. Now, two days had passed and the children still had not heard anything from him. . . . On the third day, I could not take it anymore. I told my kids that they were not going to school and I took them with me to the Bayonne police station. When I reached the station, I could not speak. I just cried and cried. I tried to tell them that FBI and immigration officers had taken my husband. They would not even listen and said very coldly, "We don't know about your husband. If the FBI took your husband we can't do anything about it. We don't know where they took him." Nobody listened to us or helped us, so I just returned home, crying.

My kids told me, "Don't cry like this. Become a strong lady." They were scared about what would happen to them. Their dad had disappeared, their mom couldn't stop crying, and no one was being sympathetic. They said, "Ask them strongly. Tell them that he has not done anything." How could I have told anyone anything when I was crying like that? I was crying at my helplessness. I was crying about how they came to my home and took my husband for no reason. I was crying because no one would tell me where he was. [*crying*]

Finally, she hired a lawyer and learned that her husband had been placed in solitary confinement at the special housing unit at the MDC in Brooklyn on grounds of an immigration violation. It took her approximately three months to arrange a personal visit with him.[15]

Many times, I found lies and hypocrisy lurking beneath the restrictions. In spring 2006 I wanted to work as a volunteer translator for Guantánamo Bay detainees. I contacted a lawyer from the Center for Constitutional Rights who was representing an Urdu-speaking detainee who required translation. The lawyer sent me a large packet of papers that I needed to fill out to receive U.S. government security clearance before I could work as a volunteer. Looking through the information packet, I felt that my political activism and my PhD in ethnic studies would likely create obstacles to getting this clearance quickly.

I called my brother Anjum, also an Urdu speaker. He had held top-secret security clearance with special compartmental information (TS-SCI), one of the highest levels of clearance, during his U.S. military career. Anjum had expressed his frustration at the "enemy combatant" status of Guantánamo Bay inmates, and as a U.S. citizen, he wanted to help. The lawyer looked quickly at Anjum's credentials and agreed that his security clearance would be easier to obtain than mine. Anjum first asked whether his previous security clearance might be sufficient, since he had held a higher level of clearance than was required for translation. The Department of Homeland Security said no.

Over two days, he compiled twenty-five years of records and submitted them for review. Three months later, a retired investigator interviewed him for half an hour in Santa Monica, California, asking routine questions about his background. After they waited several months more, the lawyer became impatient and called his own member of Congress. Eventually the lawyer was told that the first investigator did not complete the interview correctly and therefore Anjum would have to do another interview. After another month, an active-duty investigator came to interview Anjum in Ontario, California. This interview lasted for less than half an hour and Anjum went back to waiting. A couple of months later, the attorney again called the member of Congress, and with this high-powered intervention, Anjum finally got his security clearance. The lawyer and Anjum quickly booked a flight to Guantánamo Bay. While Anjum was finalizing plans for his visit, the attorney sent Anjum an e-mail reporting that the detainee had been released and sent back to his country. Translation services would not be needed.[16]

No explanation was given for the detainee's sudden release, and we may never know the real reasons. However, based on similar cases in which Guantánamo prisoners were released without explanation after years of detention, I can't help but assume that the delays in granting clearance were intended to deter outside involvement so the government could continue to frame the detainees as terrorists and justify their detention. The government knew it was holding people without any proof of wrongdoing. If anyone intervened seriously in a case, they released the person quickly since they knew that they would not be able to explain the detention. If the attorney and Anjum had not intervened in this case, the former detainee might still be counting the shadows of clouds in his cell.

Fears among Detainees in Detention and After Release

In a small village close to my hometown of Sialkot, Pakistan, I perched on the back of young Asad's motorbike as he swerved deftly to avoid potholes. Finally we arrived at the house of Bilal (a pseudonym). I asked Asad, the son of a friend of mine, to wait while I knocked on the door and introduced myself. I had received Bilal's name from a list of detainees deported to Pakistan. But he refused to talk, to give his name or any other information. His refusal did not surprise or discourage me. Throughout my research, I encountered so many hesitations, refusals, and silences that I started to understand and respect them. Bilal did not tell me the reasons for his reticence, but some other former detainees were forthright about the reasons for their hesitation.

Yasser Ebrahim, an Egyptian arrested for an expired visa and held in solitary confinement at the MDC for approximately ten months, explained why he did not want to talk about his prison experience:

> I don't know what people outside of my family think of our detention. . . . I don't know if people believe my story or not. For some people the whole situation seems strange, especially in the United States. Let's assume that I'd lived in the United States before 9/11 without any difficulties and had come back to Egypt after a few years. If somebody came from the U.S. and told me a story like this [of unjustified detention], I wouldn't believe it based on my past experiences in the United States. I would think that he was lying, that he did have some connection to the attacks but that he was denying it.[17]

Sultan Mahmood, a man in his fifties from Sialkot, told me that it did not feel good to talk about the prison experience to people in Pakistan. People there did not understand. Detention is not a pleasant experience, and it was difficult to explain that he had been placed in a high-security jail for an immigration violation. Even if people believed that the 9/11 hysteria caused enforcement officers to target Sultan, he still had an immigration violation. Some people might criticize him for breaking the law or for failing to secure a valid work permit. To avoid such questions, it was better to say that he had decided to return because conditions in the United States after 9/11 were not good for Muslims. For him, it was a question of respect:

> My older brother asked, "Was everything okay? How come we could not locate you?" I told him, "People were getting arrested so I went to another place." I did not tell my brother that I was in jail. . . . I was afraid that he would feel bad about it. . . . I don't want to tell people that I was in jail. It is an insult for me. I don't like it . . . is a question of respect and insult. . . . Sometimes, I don't want to tell even my brothers and sisters because they would make different kind of stories. They would question, "Why was he in jail?" . . . They can make stories to put you down. They would say, "Look at him, he used to brag, now look what happened to him. Look at him, he came back after spending time in jail." These are mental games that people play. . . . They already know about [my detention]. . . . When people started to get arrested, everybody in the world knew about it. They already guessed that I was arrested . . . but they don't confront me.[18]

Sultan had come to see me at my friend's house, and after a few hours his wife called to confirm that he was safe. He confessed that he had been a bit scared before meeting me. But I had grown up in Sialkot and my family had strong roots there, so I was able to share some of the family connections, gaining Sultan's acceptance and respect. By the end of the interview he was comfortable with me and gave me a few more contacts and telephone numbers.

Such lingering fear and hesitation was common among individuals who had been released and deported. Reluctance to talk was even more intense among detainees who were still inside detention centers. I met Ansar Mahmood (no relation to Anser Mahmood) at the Batavia Detention Center in Buffalo, New York, in early 2003. At that time he was fighting deportation. During my short visit, in which we spoke Punjabi, he provided me details about his case. When I asked about the attitudes of the security guards, he replied, "I can't talk about this at this time." Ansar was deported to Pakistan after fighting a fierce battle with the immigration authorities for over three years. I stayed in touch with him by phone during his detention, but he never said anything about the guards during those conversations. Often, we would switch to Punjabi when he had something to say that he did not want the administration to understand.

Only later, when I met in him in Pakistan after his release, did he go into detail about the guards. Jail administrators had used different strategies to stop him from talking to the media. One method was a strip and body cavity search. Once his case started to receive publicity, Ansar had meetings with media representatives, and after every such encounter he had to undergo a strip and cavity search. Both the security guards and Ansar knew that the purpose of these strip searches was harassment. However, Ansar felt that he could not complain about it because that would mean that the administration had achieved its purpose in intimidating him.[19]

Yaser Ebrahim was a primary plaintiff in *Turkmen v. Ashcroft*, a class action lawsuit on behalf of Arab and Muslim men rounded up in immigration sweeps after 9/11.[20] He recalled what happened when Bill Goodman, an attorney with the Center for Constitutional Rights, first approached him to join the lawsuit:

> In May 2002 while I was still at the MDC, a guard told me that a lawyer wanted to see me. I always thought that they might pin false charges on me, so I was really scared when I went to see the lawyer. The lawyer introduced himself as Mr. Bill Goodman from the Center for Constitutional Rights. He was working on a legal case against high-ranking

government officials with regards to what was happening to inmates at the MDC. He indicated that my brother and I had strong cases because we had only immigration violations and he wanted us to participate in the case. I refused at first because I was so scared. I didn't know what would happen to me after suing all those people. That was in May. "I can't do it because I am scared. My brother is by himself downstairs and I don't know what would happen to us if we joined the lawsuit," I told Mr. Goodman. "Just think about it and I will come back to you," he replied.[21]

Later, however, Yaser heard that his brother had been deported, and once he confirmed that, he worked up the courage to participate in the lawsuit. After he contacted the lawyer and offered to give a deposition, the government deported him as well.[22] In a telephone conversation, Rachel Meeropol, lead counsel on *Turkmen v. Ashcroft*, recalled the initial difficulties of locating former detainees to participate in the lawsuit.

In some situations, nongovernmental and governmental organizations looking into abuses have encountered problems getting complete information from detainees, who fear retribution if they talk. Sultan Mahmood recalled his meeting with representatives from the Office of the Inspector General (OIG), which was investigating patterns of abuse at the MDC. They asked Sultan if he had had any problems. Sultan replied, "No, everything is okay. I just need to get outside as soon as possible." He thought that talking to the inspectors might delay his deportation process.[23]

Another example is Wael Kishk. The OIG report includes a reference to his detention at the Passaic County Jail in Paterson, New Jersey, where he was transferred after six months at the Brooklyn MDC:

> One detainee spent his first four days [sic] at Passaic in the SDU [Special Detention Unit] after being transferred from the MDC on March 25, 2002. The detainee told the OIG that he was segregated because of his physical and mental condition at the time. The detainee stated that when he arrived at Passaic he was depressed, non-communicative, and could not walk after spending six months at the MDC. Passaic officials segregated him from other inmates and detainees until they could assess his condition.[24]

I showed the statement to Wael and asked him about his meeting with the OIG investigators. He said that it was very difficult to trust anyone in a detention center, especially when so many people had lied to him. How could he trust anyone who claimed that he was from the Office of the Inspector General? These individuals, although they were investigating abuse, still worked for the U.S. government.[25] Wael's loss of trust was not limited to the detention center; it was and remains pervasive. Even eight years after his release, he hesitates to trust others, including me. On my most recent phone call to him, in 2008, he was afraid that the phone line was tapped. Spending nearly a year in solitary confinement under abusive conditions has scarred him. Working with him is like walking on eggshells. I never know when he will be comfortable sharing his story and when he will have a change of heart. As a researcher and a friend, I understand that I need to provide him space, but as a writer I am never confident that I can publish his story.

Despite their nagging fears, some released detainees did talk to journalists, nongovernmental organizations, and legal organizations. Amnesty International published its first memo on the detentions in November 2001, exposing the prevalence of racial profiling, prolonged arbitrary detentions, and lack of legal access.[26] Human Rights Watch issued a report at the beginning of 2002 that included detailed testimonies of detainees stuck in jails.[27] In response to detainees' complaints, the Office of the Inspector General started its investigation and a year later published two reports confirming that the government had used immigration violations as a pretext to detain individuals from Muslim communities.[28]

Certain detainees' cases were so well publicized that they did not have the option of hiding them. I met Azmath Mohammad at the Hudson County Correctional Center in Kearny, New Jersey, in December 2002. At that time he was about to be deported. Separated from him by a glass door and talking through a telephone, I kept my conversation with him simple and brief. I did not ask him detailed questions because I felt that he would not be able to answer them in those circumstances. I asked if I could visit him after his release, and he gave me his address and phone number in India.

When I went to see Azmath at his house in Hyderabad, India, he greeted me with open arms. He had a burning desire to tell his story and describe to the world the abuse that he had suffered for more than a year while being held on the ninth floor of the MDC, purportedly for an immigration violation. He expressed fear of what the Indian and U.S. governments might do to him even after his deportation. However, his desire to seek justice outweighed his fear. He gave interviews to CNN, BBC, and many other media networks. His wife, Tasleem, was a bit more cautious in her choice of words and refrained from directly criticizing the U.S. government.

On the other hand, I had difficulty making contact with Azmath's friend, Ayub Khan, who was arrested with him and suffered similar abuse. Ayub refused to talk to me in India, even though he had invited me to visit him in response to the letter that I wrote him while he was at the detention center. During my stay in India, I left him several messages. A few years later, when I sent Azmath a draft of his story, Ayub also read it. He sent me an e-mail and asked me to write his story too. In early 2003, he may not have trusted me, but by 2007, having read Azmath's narrative, he was inspired to share his own experience. Throughout my research, it was impossible to predict how individuals would respond. Some set up meetings on the phone and then never showed up. Some rescheduled several times. Some would give their stories only after I promised not to publish their names. Some agreed to have the story included in the dissertation but not in the book. Some would share certain portions of their stories but not others.

A number of Egyptian nationals suffered further mistreatment in Egyptian jails after being deported from the United States. Even today, years after the fact, some refuse to describe their suffering in Egyptian detention centers. They do not have any other place to go and they do not want to create additional enemies in the only country they can consider home.

In doing oral history with detainees and former detainees, I have to keep the narrators' safety paramount. Any recorded conversation could be used in a court of law, where it could be manipulated to play on public fears of terror attacks and of people with certain ethnic and religious backgrounds. I know that I can't publish certain comments even though the narrators spoke on record and signed consent forms. In some situations, I used my judgment and deleted from the record a statement that I though could put the person under surveillance. In addition, because almost all the former detainees had legal cases, I asked Rachel Meeropol from the Center for Constitutional Rights to read the stories, and she asked for minor changes to ensure their safety.

Raheem (a pseudonym), a released detainee in Egypt, gave me interesting details about how he created a fake passport in France and entered the United States several times under fictitious identities. During his detention at the Passaic County Jail, security guards severely beat him for insisting on eating a nonvegetarian meal when he had signed up for vegetarian meals. Several of his fellow detainees witnessed his swollen face, blackened eyes, and inability to walk for weeks. Raheem filed a complaint with the authorities and his case was included in the OIG report.

Raheem had an interesting immigration history, and I thought about including his narrative in my book. However, I decided against it because I felt that most readers would not care about the injustices he had suffered on trumped-up terrorism charges—after all, he had dodged the legal immigration system many times. Raheem's story could have contributed to the history of immigration, showing how individuals use creative strategies to come to the United States for better economic opportunities and how they love America for the economic opportunities it provides. But I did not want to jeopardize his legal case by presenting information that might be seen in a negative light.

Dissociation from Family and Friends

After Uzma Naheed's husband, Anser Mahmood, was arrested and taken to the MDC in New York, she tried to call people within the local Pakistani and Muslim community for help. The overwhelming majority of them reacted with indifference. Sometimes they would not even pick up the phone. When they did, they did not want to talk about it. "We can't discuss this issue with you," was a common response.

While Uzma felt abandoned and alone during this time of need, she understood why her neighbors sought to dissociate themselves. Pakistani and Muslim communities were under surveillance, and people feared that they might get into trouble with the FBI if they talked to her. Uzma herself had gotten into trouble when her brother was arrested for an immigration violation. While investigating her brother, the FBI came to her house and found that Uzma and her husband also had immigration violations. Since Uzma was nursing a newborn, they arrested only her husband.[29]

Several other former detainees and their family members also complained that their friends did not talk to them, cut off the relationship, and became strangers. This dissociation was painful for detainees and their families, but they understood it as an issue of survival. Neighbors and friends knew there was little they could do to help someone targeted by the authorities, and no one wanted to risk being questioned and detained.

Ansar Mahmood, his friend Tabeeb, and Tabeeb's wife Shaheena were arrested together in Hudson, New York, in early October 2001, after Ansar snapped a photo of a scenic view that happened to contain a water reservoir. Ansar had a valid green card, but both Tabeeb and his wife Shaheena (pseudonyms) had expired visas and had used fictitious names to gain work permits. Ansar was charged with helping undocumented immigrants obtain jobs and an apartment and was released on bail in late October.

Shaheena stayed in a local jail while waiting for her deportation. Her husband was in a different immigration jail and they could not talk to each other except by sending letters through the mail. Ansar was Shaheena's only real friend in the outside world. He was concerned about her happiness and safety and received her collect calls on a frequent basis. However, Ansar had a pending legal case himself. His attorney advised him to stop talking with Shaheena because his telephone lines could be tapped and immigration authorities could use their conversations to strengthen the legal case against Ansar. Reluctantly, Ansar told Shaheena that it would be better if she did not call him. During my interview with Shaheena, she vividly remembered the pain of losing her lifeline to the outside and facing isolation in that dark cell.[30] Ansar admitted with anguish that he had to put his own safety first.[31]

I felt similar pain and conflict during a visit to my relative's house in Pakistan. My relative told me about one of her friends, a doctor, who had been arrested in Pakistan for doing volunteer medical work in Afghanistan. While staying at her house, I told my relative about my research and expressed interest in talking to the doctor's family. We were in the process of arranging the visit when Pakistani intelligence agents, accompanied by Americans (local newspapers reported that they were FBI agents), raided the doctor's house. They arrested his sons and took his computers and all of the paperwork from the house and the adjoining clinic. After this raid, my relative and her family feared for their own safety. Their names and contacts could easily be found in the doctor's records and now they also could be easily raided and investigated. I could see the anguish on their faces as they told me that they couldn't call their family friends at that time. Staying with them, I felt the trauma that comes in cutting your friends off to protect yourself and your family.

Self-Surveillance and Loss of Trust

The oral histories I collected from detainees and deportees revealed how the government manipulated information to harass vulnerable individuals. Innocent young men were turned into suspects because of their ethnic and racial background, and enforcement officers used every means to entrap and unfairly incarcerate them.

During my public talks, some people have asked, "Are you afraid that the FBI may be watching you?" My first response has been, "No, I don't think the FBI is watching me," or "No, I am not under surveillance."

While I'm not certain if anyone is watching me or not, since 2001 I have been watching myself and being careful what I say about political issues in public. I could easily be stopped because of my looks, and depending on the mood of the enforcement officer, anything in my possession could be considered suspect. I could find myself behind bars or sent to an undisclosed location while the government searches for connections with al-Qaeda. While I would surely be released eventually, I would lose time on my work and I would be stigmatized. This fear keeps me on edge, especially during my international travels, when I must talk to immigration and customs officials.

While I am vulnerable because of my ethnicity, I'm aware that my academic credentials, my association with a well-known university, my gender, and my U.S. citizenship provide me some protection. My research revealed a pattern: enforcement officers tend to target vulnerable individuals, typically noncitizen males with minor immigration violations. I asked my partner, an Egyptian artist then in the United States on a temporary visa, to prepare a scale model of the ninth floor of the MDC for an art exhibit. He smiled and asked, "Do you want me to stay there?" I had seen his political work in Egypt, some of which was critical of U.S. policies in the Middle East. Many times I asked him to prepare similar pieces for an exhibit in the United States. He never did. I understood his hesitance and realized that the time we are living in is one of repression, when free expression can endanger personal safety.

I believe that the stories of the people arrested, detained, or deported on flimsy pretexts after 9/11 are stories that need to be told. I don't want to stop asking questions, making telephone calls, or writing. But there is a degree of self-imposed censorship, both in my writing and in what I say about my writing. This self-censorship stems from the fact that the state has been secretive around these detentions under the name of national security. The mainstream media has generally presented the government's position, that is, that the individuals arrested after 9/11 had some connection with terrorism or at a minimum were "illegals," and therefore the government had the legal right to detain and deport them. In the so-called war on terror, the arbitrary detentions of a few thousand individuals are justified in the pursuit of national security; the loss of civil liberties becomes mere collateral damage. Muslim bodies have been made disposable, much like the black "surplus population" of the prison-industrial complex.[32]

Notes

1. United States of America v. Wael Kishk, USDC CR-01-1092, United States District Court for the Eastern District of New York, January 14, 2002, trial transcript, 80–81.

2. Trial transcripts give the names of both prospective jurors. One acknowledges her Muslim heritage and the other's name confirms his Muslim background.

3. Irum Shiekh, Being Muslim in America (working title) (New York: Palgrave Macmillan, forthcoming).

4. Some told me that their applications for U.S. citizenship faced deeper scrutiny because of their ethnic and religious backgrounds. Some experienced unusual delays, and in some cases the government completed additional background investigations despite the fact that these immigrants already held valid green cards.

5. Casey Peek and Irum Shiekh, Hidden Internment: The Art Shibayama Story (Progressive Films, 2004).

6. American-Arab Anti-Discrimination Committee, Report on Hate Crimes & Discrimination against Arab Americans: The Post-September 11 Backlash: September 11, 2001 to October 11, 2002 (Washington DC: American-Arab Anti-Discrimination Committee Research Institute, 2003), 43, 69. Sikhs are of South Asian origin but they are not Muslim.

7. Anjum Shiekh, interview by author, South Beach, Florida, October 25 and December 12, 2001.

8. I use the term *vulnerable* to indicate the government strategy of targeting those Muslim and Muslim-looking persons with the least protection from state harassment, mainly noncitizen immigrants with minor immigration violations.

9. Michael Truman, e-mails to author, July 2 and December 10, 2007, and January 18, January 23, and January 24, 2008.

10. I sent the letter to Wanda M. Hunt, Chief, FOIA/PA Section, Federal Bureau of Prisons, on November 18, 2007.

11. Office of the Inspector General, U.S. Department of Justice, Supplemental Report on September 11 Detainees' Allegations of Abuse at the Metropolitan Detention Center in Brooklyn, New York (Washington, DC, December 2003).

12. The letter from Wanda M. Hunt, Chief, FOIA/PA Section, Federal Bureau of Prisons, is dated December 12, 2008.

13. The lawyer, Michael D. Steger, sent the letter to the Office of Information and Privacy, U.S. Department of Justice, on February 5, 2009.

14. United States Senate Committee on the Judiciary, "Testimony of Gerald Goldstein, Attorney, National Association of Criminal Defense Lawyers, DOJ Oversight: Preserving Our Freedom While Defending against Terrorism," Washington, DC, December 4, 2001.

15. Uzma Naheed, interview by author, Lahore, Pakistan, February 23, 2003.

16. Anjum Shiekh, e-mail to author, February 15, 2008.

17. Yasser Ebrahim, interview by author, Alexandria, Egypt, April 23, 2003.

18. Sultan Mahmood, interview by author, Sialkot, Pakistan, February 11, 2003.

19. Ansar Mahmood, interview by author, Islamabad, Pakistan, November 19, 2005.

20. An update on *Turkmen v. Ashcroft* is available on the website of the Center for Constitutional Rights, http://ccrjustice.org/ourcases/current-cases/turkmen-v.-ashcroft.

21. Yaser Ebrahim, interview by author, Alexandria, Egypt, April 23, 2003.

22. Yasser Ebrahim, interview by author, Alexandria, Egypt, April 23, 2003.

23. Sultan Mahmood, interview by author, Sialkot, Pakistan, February 11, 2003.

24. Office of the Inspector General, U.S. Department of Justice, The September 11 Detainees: A Review of the Treatment of Aliens Held on Immigration Charges in Connection with the Investigation of the September 11 Attacks (Washington, DC, 2003), 171. Wael spent over four months at Passaic in the Special Detention Unit.

25. Wael Kishk, interview by author, Cairo, Egypt, December 5, 2008.

26. Amnesty International, "United States of America: Memorandum to the US Attorney General—Amnesty International's concerns relating to the post–11 September investigations," AMR 51/170/2001, November 1, 2001.

27. Human Rights Watch, Presumption of Guilt: Human Rights Abuses of Post–September 11 Detainees (Washington, DC: Human Rights Watch, 2002).

28. Office of the Inspector General, U.S. Department of Justice, The September 11 Detainees; Office of the Inspector General, U.S. Department of Justice, Supplemental Report on September 11 Detainees' Allegations of Abuse at the Metropolitan Detention Center in Brooklyn, New York (Washington, DC, December 2003).

29. Uzma Naheed, interview by author, Lahore, Pakistan, February 23, 2003.

30. Shaheena, interview by author, February 15, 2003.

31. Ansar Mahmood, interview by author, Pakistan, November 19, 2005.

32. Christian Parenti, Lockdown America: Police and Prisons in the Age of Crisis (New York: Verso, 1999).

33. Some Muslim feminist scholars are already working toward it, and I congratulate them for their courage and determination.

Capturing the Reflective Voice
An Interview with Karen Mary Davalos

Conducted by Teresa Barnett and Chon A. Noriega, June 2009

NORIEGA: Karen Mary, maybe if you could just start and say a little bit about your training in oral history research, particularly the disciplinary framework for that, and give us some sense of the work that you've done.

DAVALOS: I have to admit that my training as a cultural anthropologist wasn't specifically in oral history. I mean, anthropologists think they're the experts on how to do an interview. But we borrow from folklorists and others who use oral history as the method. We would see it as one of many methods. Nothing really changes in the type of interview you're doing. You have to have a strong rapport with the person you're interviewing. You have to have a very solid sense of where they're coming from, what their past is, and how they relate it to the project. You have to have a very clear sense of the objective of the interview. And then you have to be, you know, good anthropologists; we all think we're the experts at this. You know that you'll be able to fly by the seat of your pants because everything you thought you knew could go out the window two seconds into the interview. Flexibility was really the strength of the training.

I think what I learned along the way, though, in cultural anthropology—this is like mid-'80s, early '90s, right? My training was at Yale. I think what I learned along the way is that collaborative research is what is really valuable. So what I say about my training in Chicano/Chicana anthropology is that I learned it in the hallway, okay? There wasn't a specific class I could take. Especially when I got to Yale, there were only one or two professors who could teach anything on Chicano studies, Chicano subject matter. But I was talking in the hallways with other students and going to conferences. So there wasn't any formal training.

But what I was getting in this Chicano anthropology was to be always invested in collaboration with the people at the center of the research. What I brought to my training in anthropology was an understanding about the person you're interviewing. The interviewee must agree to and have some control over the questions—over the direction you're going to take in the interview. It's not acceptable to spring it on them at the last minute. Prior to the actual interview, the person and I would collaborate on the nature and direction of the interview. And of course that was oral history. That was the methodology of oral history, that you set up the pre-interview. Before you sit down to turn on the tape recorder there is that pre-interview where you go through questions like, "This is what I want to cover. Would this be suitable? What am I missing?" And so that was my formal training. It really was through anthropological methods and thinking that anthropologists were the experts but then realizing that they were missing a key ingredient, a collaborative approach.

NORIEGA: Now, at this time, anthropology is changing somewhat from a colonial model where you interview people who are different than you to something that's at one point called auto-ethnographic. So what's at stake in terms of you as an anthropologist interviewing other Latinos—

DAVALOS: What's at stake?

NORIEGA: Within a contemporary urban environment, I mean.

DAVALOS: I was at an institution that didn't even value that yet, right? It was still, "Why do you want to go to Chicago? Why don't you go to Mexico to study identity?" So I wasn't getting support. I was reading José Limón, Renato Rosaldo, and Martha Menchaca (she was a classmate of mine at Stanford). I was reading these folks that were doing auto-ethnography but there was never any value placed on that kind of work. By the time I finished my dissertation, I realized there's this project called "decolonial anthropology" that challenges the entire methodology and epistemology of cultural anthropology. It acknowledges that working with people like yourself is itself a new field of study and you can actually name it rather than dismiss it. So I'm not sure if that answers your question, but that's the field's concern.

The other challenge of this type of research is the people you walk into the room with, right? Like the people I want to interview. And they don't have any of those questions in their head, but they have similar questions. And I've tried to write about this, although very unsuccessfully. I'm too dark-skinned. I'm not dark enough. My Spanish is too good, I learned it in college, right? It's very formal. I use all of the wrong words—and I don't mean formal as in *usted* versus *tu* but as in using the subjunctive when no one would use the subjunctive. "Quisiera hablar con Estela." No one says that on the telephone. They don't—so I get a giggle, right? My color is wrong, my Spanish is a little off. So maybe I'm not really from California, maybe I'm from Mexico City. So there's a class tension. All of those things are what's in the room. And in fact, because I picked Chicago as a place to do research and not L.A., right, or not Southern California, not Northern California, some parts of Texas or Denver, Colorado. Because I picked this place where there's not decades of Chicanitos running around in the field, I don't get even a lot of the distrust of the university professor. It's just complete awe that someone is interested in their life. So that's what's in the room.

BARNETT: How does that awe work for you or against you in the interview?

DAVALOS: I certainly make it work for me. I have to admit I'm not afraid to take on a different persona, depending on the interview. Like the naïve younger woman, [that persona was available to me during] all of the situations during my dissertation research. I'm only twenty-something, so when I spoke with elderly women or women who are in their early thirties, I have to show them culturally a kind of respect. The younger women, the ones that are having their quinceañeras or just had, or they're sisters of ones that are younger than me—I can help the younger women by helping them think about their future. I can play the role of the mentor just by asking them questions and encouraging them to think and reflect about the quinceañera. So I would take on these personas, but never [fake it].

The challenge when doing auto-ethnography is never to play the status card. I was poorer than most of the people I was interviewing in Chicago during the dissertation research. They would give me their TV set. The women I came to know for my research would buy me jackets at the secondhand store. They would show me where to get inexpensive food and clothes for the interview. I was originally situated with a job-training and service organization. And these women that I met and eventually interviewed all had to wear that monkey suit, right? Blue vest and skirt, white shirt with a little red scarf for a female, right? Since I was participating in the job-training program, I too had to wear the suit but I could barely afford to buy clothes. And the women told me which secondhand stores are inexpensive in addition to discount stores such as Ross Dress for

Less, TJ Maxx. They knew I had no money. And yet they knew I had this cultural capital. They wouldn't use that language. The women knew that I had immense cultural capital in my future. So it was playing the type of person who could be so incredibly humble. And I learned to eat meat again during research so that the interview would go—I was a vegetarian, but I changed, and I don't see anything wrong with that. I think that's being a good interviewer. For example, I took the bus, and I wasn't ashamed to ride the bus. Because if I was ashamed that I took the bus or made less money or had no money or couldn't afford this or that, then what are they going to feel? People who are literally stuck in that low working-class economy.

So the only time I played smarter than somebody else—it occurred to me when you asked about the awe. He was an older man, at least in his sixties, and a deacon at the church, and he had organized many Via Crucis [Way of the Cross] ceremonies in Pilsen [a Chicago neighborhood with a large Mexican population]. And he was going to teach me about the Via Crucis and what it was all about. He had these religious cards with the stations of the cross. And it was in a little three-ring binder and he was going to catechize me, whatever the word is. He was going to take me through it. It was a lesson. "This is the first station, this is what it's about." And his lesson consisted of reading me the text on the cards in Spanish. First I thought, okay, this is because he thinks I'm a stupid idiot and my Spanish is bad. And then I realized that's what this man does. He's trying to convince me like he does his colleagues, the other leaders in the parish, how you're supposed to do a Via Crucis because they've gotten it all wrong, you know. "Christ is wearing a red cape with the blue lining and a cup made of gold. His chalice was gold. And that's what we have to duplicate in the ceremony, in this ritual." And so then I realized, you know what? I'm just going to tell this guy in my crooked Spanish that he did not sound like a Catholic. He sounded like a fundamentalist.

NORIEGA: So, how'd that go?

DAVALOS: We argued. He loved it. He loved the debate, and for years I would listen to the tape. I finally gave it to a student and said, "Can you transcribe this? Tell me if my Spanish is any good." "There's nothing wrong with your Spanish, Dr. Davalos. Your Spanish is fine." But the deacon, he held his own. I didn't; I was terrible. But I kept trying to challenge him and he just kept giving me, you know, "This is the way it is, we have these religious paintings for a reason." And how could I go against that? It would be going against the church. He was a fundamentalist, but raised Catholic, so . . .

NORIEGA: This raises the question if there are any distinct considerations with respect to interviewing in the Latino community when it comes to religion or spirituality.

DAVALOS: Yes, let's stick with Chicanos, because we can expand this to Latinos, but first let's just talk about Mexican-origin people in the United States. They are rarely going to talk about themselves in terms of the institutional church. And they even have a whole language around that: "Oh, we didn't go to church very much," and it's said apologetically. Or "We weren't very religious," or, "My grandmother was very involved in the church, she went to church every day." So they have this language that means that they are not involved in the church, but Latino scholars know otherwise. And it's ironic because it's as if they've read every single document on European American religious practice that talks about "devotionality" in terms of going to church.

And here I'll be general, I'll talk about most Latinos in the U.S. They are very spiritual, but they don't talk about it as religiosity, or being religious, or being associated with an institution. Even unschooled folks will have a language where they make a distinction between their spirituality and their faith. "I have a lot of faith." "Tengo mucha fe." But they would never call themselves religious. Being religious is about going to church and being involved in the church as a deacon, as a priest, as a brother, as someone who helps out with the mass. Ironically, even women I would interview both in Chicago, in formal interviews, but also talking to folks in L.A., and when I'd give a talk somewhere like San Antonio or Austin, the women might be involved with the church but they won't name that.

So it gets back to what kinds of practices. Are they involved in sacramental practices? No, they're involved in Latino Catholicism. You know, the presentation of the youth, their third month or third year or third week or whatever, it's usually around three. In immigrant communities they still do that. The quinceañera, the Via Crucis, las Posadas, all of these things that we know make up Latino spirituality. So they'll be involved in that, but they might even say they're still not very religious. They make a clear distinction between spirituality and religiosity—between popular religion and institutional religion. From what I can tell it is very Catholic, because you can't be Pentecostal and not be religious. You're either Pentecostal or you're not, right? So then you don't talk to people about religion. Even if you say to people, "Are you Catholic?" "Yes, I was raised Catholic, but . . ." I just back completely away from any of that language. Also, some people aren't married in the church and that's with good reason; maybe there was no pastor, or they didn't want to pay the cost. This is a reality among recent immigrants or even second-generation folks.

So people were very clear about the word *faith*. They have strong faith and that usually meant a reference to the sacred and the divine that was not church-based. It did not depend on church authority, and it did not require church authority for this practice or this belief. Any of the interviews I ever did with folks in the "area of religion," I would begin with a preliminary interview to map out where we were going to go. It turned into the interview. And so these folks, especially the older women, were incredibly reflective on their spirituality and faith. And that's when I started to tell myself, "Okay, don't even talk about the church." So I'd go into the home, if I was lucky enough [to be invited]—because sometimes I would interview at the parish hall—but if I was lucky enough to go into someone's home it just started with the altar. "Who's this? Where'd you get this image? Where'd you get this statue?" And it would be the pathway to the oral history. I didn't call it that at that time, but that's what these women were so eager to convey, how they had developed this intense faith, a daily recognition of the sacred in their homes and how they had learned it from elders: "That's what grandma did, that's what mother did, or uncle did or grandpa did." Somebody had this altar. And that's just the way you did it. You didn't need to go to church.

NORIEGA: Did you tape record the pre-interviews?

DAVALOS: At first I didn't but after a while, yes. I'd bring the tape recorder and I'd say, "Is it okay if I take out the machine, I have my tape recorder here?" And usually, you know, these elder women, we're talking forty to seventy-five years old, I had already made it into their homes. They were quite comfortable with me by then. There was not a hiccup. But even the younger people, I was noticing, were very accepting of the machine. So here are the twenty-somethings who I would usually talk to about quinceañeras, and who, to be blunt, didn't have a wealth of experience, right? They were young. They still were eager to talk. Even the interview that I did that's partially transcribed and published, with the girl I call Victoria, who had been planning her sister's quinceañera. She said, "Oh, I don't know anything about the quinceañera." And then she'd tell me about the quinceañera, go on and on and on, you know, hours of tape. So I was finding these women were incredibly eager to tell their story. I don't think they ever thought it had value until somebody—I wasn't the only person, but somebody came around asking.

NORIEGA: But if you approached them in terms of an institutional understanding of religion or faith, then—

DAVALOS: I think that's what let me get as far as I did in Chicago, doing the stuff on the quinceañeras, the Via Crucis, and las Posadas. Because I wasn't affiliated with the church. They would see me at masses and they would hear from me that I went to the parish over there and I went to the one over here. In Pilsen, there's like nine parishes in their community, maybe five now if they've closed some. But they knew I was going to different places, so I wasn't affiliated with one. And that probably helped me. Now that goes against everything anthropology is going to teach you. You have to go in and talk to the head man, the medicine man of the community, to write old-fashioned colonial anthropology, and that's going to be your entrée. Well, I didn't make connection with the parish leadership until much later in my research. By then I already had these connections with these women, and I went back to do more follow-up work on the Via Crucis and the Resurrection Project, a Catholic faith-based community development corporation. I knew people who were in both organizations: those who were organizing the stations of the cross, the celebration or commemoration for Good Friday, and also building homes in the low-income communities of Pilsen and Little Village. I didn't need an entrée from a priest. And when I started naming priests later, I always found that got me into trouble. Name a nun and that was okay, but name a priest and that was just . . . even priests I thought were low-key and that people would have no reason to dislike them. One or two of them were very controversial, they were known for *x*, *y*, and *z* or whatever, but for the others, I think it was a gender dynamic. Not just the institutional church. The priests that I know well, we actually kept our relationship separate from the research so that it wouldn't interfere.

BARNETT: Did the women ever actually criticize the church, too?

DAVALOS: Oh yes, oh yes. And you know, this was before all the pedophilia crisis and cover-up. During my dissertation research in Chicago the archdiocese was closing parishes because of lack of funds. The Archdiocese of Chicago closed twenty-two parishes in the city in a one- or two-year period. And so the women's critique was incredible. They understood the historical and race-based and gender-based dimensions; they could see many dimensions, not just the typical conflicts. "He's a hypocrite because he does *x*, *y*, and *z*"—that is what people usually are going to get into. But I also made it very clear that I wasn't interested in that. I wanted to hear their stories, and when you continue on that line for so long, people really see that you're genuine about that. Like, "What did you do with your quinceañera? What did that medallion your grandmother gave to you mean?" I always loved Clifford Gertz's argument about "thick description." And there's no such thing as thin description. There's just bad questions. So I've done some pretty rotten interviews over my time, but, you know, people have a story to tell. It's very, very dear to them. All you have to do is ask the right questions. And so when it comes to religion, it's important to avoid any language that is going to frame the question. And don't frame a question that's about the church as an institution. It has to be about spirituality and faith. Expressions of faith can take place in any setting, and anybody can be an authority.

NORIEGA: Are there other aspects of doing oral history within the Latino or Chicano community where [taking a position rooted in] mainstream middle-class American society is not going to yield discussion? I'm wondering if maybe the same thing happens with education. We, as a society, tend to think of education in terms of institutions and formal schooling.

DAVALOS: Yes, yes, because when I think back on those earliest interviews—I'm probably going to contradict myself, but there were moments in Chicago, and I've seen it elsewhere, like here in Los Angeles, when you mention that you go to Yale or have a degree and you're getting another degree, that's going to influence the interview. But what I did was I made it very clear that I valued my grandmother's education, and so I would start it off with a story about myself. There was always a moment where I would get the litmus test: "Where are you from?" Because I wasn't from Chicago, right? So I was given the litmus test and my background was quite wrong. But I found that if I talked about my grandmother being a third-grade educated woman who taught herself to read and write in Spanish and English, that was important to people. That meant a lot, right? That she was *bien educada*, a well-educated person.

But the point that would really form the relationship for people I was talking to is the story about my grandmother's name. My grandmother spelled her name Davalos, no accent. "No lleva acento sobre la *a*." You know, you just don't do that. She didn't know about accents that were written in. So I would tell them, "This is how you spell my name." And I don't put the accent out of respect for my grandmother. And so people who were less "formally educated"—in quotes, right, "formally educated"—they found that as an entrée point to talk to me, whereas my colleagues all want to correct it: "No, you have to fix that because Grandma was making a mistake." I was like, "Are you kidding?"

I think there are probably multiple institutions that claim authority, not just in education, not just in religion. You could think of health, right? We have health systems within the Latino community that are independent of the society's health care system, and they continue to operate and function among third-generation, fourth-generation Latinos. My student, for example, has been writing about *curanderismo*, and she makes a statement in her thesis, in the first sentence of her thesis, that it's something that is part of a Mexican American home. And I thought to myself, "Okay, that's overstatement." But then she starts to give examples. And so, my grandmother came over—I can't remember how social scientists distinguish the generations, it's different for social scientists in different fields—but my grandmother was born in Mexico, my father was born here, his first language is Spanish. My first language is mostly English and by the time I get to high school, that's all I speak. We were given tea for an upset stomach, we were told never to talk lovingly about a baby unless you're touching it. I'm trying to think of another example of our cultural health system.

These are all healing practices, part of that spiritual faith-health system, right? It is an integrated faith-health system. I think you could probably think of many examples. What I'm saying is you don't even have to assume this is about a Latino immigrant population; it's not simply or strictly the first and second generations. Even among third and fourth generation Latinos, you have to be careful in your language. And sometimes more careful because of the anxiety and the guilt about their cultural heritage in the context of anti-immigrant attitudes and racism, or whatever cultural code you want to identify that people might have but because they haven't succeeded in those institutions of health, education, and religion, they will not talk with you about such topics. I'm trying to help you figure out what are the other ones would be, but those are the first three that come to mind: health, religion, education.

NORIEGA: That's interesting because it seems like you could ask somebody, "Do you believe in curanderos?" "No way."

DAVALOS: The Chicano fourth generation is going to think you're nuts. They're going to be like, "That's what my grandmother did or believed."

NORIEGA: But then if you ask them about their day-to-day practices, you might find out something a little bit different.

DAVALOS: Right. I ask my students, "Who has an altar in their family?" Nobody raises their hand. "Do you have a special place in the house that grandma said never touch it and it had these kinds of things on it: family pictures, mementos from somebody's quinceañera or wedding or graduation ceremonies, or religious pictures or statues, maybe a Virgen de Guadalupe or Christ on the crucifix?" "Oh yes, we had that right on top of the TV." "Who dusted it? Who kept it clean?" "Oh, I never did as a kid." "Who did?" "Must've been grandma." Everybody has that, you know.

BARNETT: That example also speaks to the importance of interviewing in people's homes—when you said you could be at their home and actually point to things.

DAVALOS: Oh yes, and the same for quinceañeras, because imagine, I was meeting people of all ages—the eighteen-year-old who had completed her quinceañera, the young women in their twenties, and the mothers who helped plan their daughters' quinceañeras. I probably wasn't meeting a lot of fifteen-year-olds, right? They're in school. So what do we do? We take out the photo album. Now today it's going to be a little bit different, given digital cameras, you can't really rely on the presence of the album, but you could use the video cam, the video, the VCR to look at and say, "So who's that, how are they related?" and ta-da. You could go on for hours, two, three hours, people are going to tell you about that event. So all kinds of stuff is available to researchers if they're paying attention to the family's method of documenting. And this is an organic method to the family, something familiar and natural to them. So it's got another layer of how they reflect on their lives, their spirituality, their community. "So who didn't come to the party, who wasn't allowed to be invited?" It even gives you the missing information. The worry in oral history is "Oh well, it's only showing what the lens captured, it's narrowing the field." No, it opens up! You've got this rich thing—the video or the pictures—and then over here that's what's left out. And you're going to learn things about the family. "No, you can't invite that cousin because he got into a fight with so-and-so at the last quinceañera, and so my mother said he's too dangerous." You're not going to get that story if you're not paying attention to who's in the picture and who's not.

BARNETT: I have a question, maybe returning to religion a little bit more, with regard to you as an interviewer. Religion is particular, spirituality in particular is seen to be such a personal matter, and I wondered how they thought of you that way. Did you share their spirituality, and how did that play into their sense of you?

DAVALOS: Yes, this is probably good old-fashioned field methods. An American anthropologist, I can't remember what his name was, said everybody should go into psychotherapy before they go into the field. You could probably look it up, but good old-fashioned American anthropological methods—he was a contemporary of Kroeber, if I recall. Well, I realized he was absolutely right. I had to become very much in touch with who I was as a spiritual person. Some of that started in the field right away, because you're in Chicago and nobody says "Chicano." A Chicano is a person who's stuck up with their nose in the air, out of touch, doesn't understand the community, thinks they're better than everybody else, and is trying to speak perfect Spanish or something, whatever. So I am not a Chicano. I just started to realize I had to figure out who I was before I could ask a question.

NORIEGA: A Mexican.

DAVALOS: I became a Mexicana, short story. Became a Mexicana-slash-Chicana; I learned that very quickly when I got back to California. So I had to figure out my own spirituality. And I think for me that wasn't a very difficult thing to do, because I was raised Catholic and many of these things were very familiar to me. I understood in my college years that no matter what was wrong with the institutional church, everybody needs, I profoundly believe that everybody needs an understanding of the divine. And that's how I learned mine. That was not hard to share, and I also learned this informally. In fact, I guess it would be the opposite of my academic training, and it was probably the stuff you learned in the hallway, right, along with the Chicano anthropology and the decolonial methodologies. I could not walk away from this community. I was investing my own relationships, and so that whole "objective," in quotes, "objective" social scientist—I knew I was never that.

But I also didn't pretend I was the native. They were very clear on this fact—that I didn't belong and they didn't want me to stay; I had opportunities. They were not being cruel; they were just like, "You're out of here." So I lived in Chicago two and a half years and came back many times, but the first time I came back with the dissertation in hand and shared it with everyone. I tried to keep in touch with the younger women. That was very hard; it was only the older people who were settled down that I still have some contact with. I went to baptisms, went to quinceañeras, went to mass with them, went to wakes—you know, someone had a grandmother died and prayed the rosary, what is that called? The nine days of a novena. Is that what it is?

NORIEGA: You're the anthropologist. [*laughter*]

DAVALOS: I know this but I don't, you know, have personal or prior experience with every ritual. I knew you'd go to the rosary. It wasn't just that you go to the wake and the funeral, that's one thing, but it was the nine days of praying the rosary on my knees with my partner there. You know, my white gringo partner praying in Spanish. I mean that wasn't hard for me, the Posadas in the freezing cold. That wasn't hard for me. If they were trying to test me, I didn't get a sense of that, if that's what you mean.

BARNETT: Did you ever interview anybody whose spirituality—well, you talked about the guy with the cards, but did you ever interview someone on spiritual matters where you felt a kind of consonance with that tradition and that faith? You may not see it exactly as they do, but I always think about how academics do so poorly when they interview on religion, often, because they may not fundamentally agree with that person, particularly on religion. So I've seen interviews with fundamentalists and so forth where it's just like, kind of raise the question, do we move on or whatever? And I wonder if you've ever interviewed someone whose religiosity, spirituality, felt fundamentally different from yours, and what that was like?

DAVALOS: I could tell you I met a lot of younger girls who would say that they weren't like their parents. But they wore a cross around their neck, or the Virgin of Guadalupe or something. And that's what I mean by "thick and thin description." I just hadn't found the right questions to ask them. Because that necklace, that medallion never came off. Okay, so was it representing a relationship with somebody who gave it to them? Why that necklace or image? Why would they wear it? I guess no, I hadn't—I probably met one family that was not Catholic, and they did not really talk a lot during the interview. I'm trying to remember this, maybe that was it. They were not Catholic; they had changed denominations and had become Pentecostal. Most of the family members I was talking to were Catholics, and the non-Catholics were less present. . . . But then, yes, in some ways a lot of people self-select and become part of the research because they can see themselves in the project that I describe or the types of topics that I am interested in.

NORIEGA: Follow-up question to that: just given that we come from an enterprise that tends to be secular or agnostic, why is it important to know about religion?

DAVALOS: I don't think you could understand Mexican-origin people living in the United States without understanding their spirituality. I think it would be a huge gap. There is so much that is about the divine and the sacred, and how the divine is present in everyday experience. I think Mexican-origin people are deeply spiritual, and to not talk about that would be to misunderstand their everyday experience and worldviews. I'm not the first one to say it. Davíd Carrasco has been trying to convince Chicano studies to expand its topics for a long time. What I've learned is that so many things are connected to spirituality that it's just a profound part of everyday experience. The health system, the way we think about wellness and illness, the way we think about relationships. This can be said for other Latino groups, the ones that I know from the literature: Cuban, Puerto Rican, Dominican, Central and South American. I mean it's just so profoundly true. There's no embarrassment about accepting a greater being. So, how could you not talk about it?

NORIEGA: But it seems like at the same time, you're engaging people where the theological dimension has perhaps been lost over the course of a generation or two, or the formal understanding of that.

DAVALOS: In Mexico people aren't churched. They don't rely on the church for their spiritual experience. They have to go to and pay a priest for the sacraments, and not every town, not every small village has a parish. There's been a shortage of parish priests in Mexico longer than there has been in the U.S. and Canada, so it's a very different experience with spiritual matters. And the institutional church, you know, has a negative—in Mexico it's part of the problem, right? For *la gente* it can be corrupt. It's part of the system of oppression.

The church and its power is not a reason to avoid research on the topic. I'm talking about spirituality, a sense of the divine. The question is this: Is it Catholic? And that's what the religious scholars and the theologians actually debate. Okay, curanderismo. But is it Catholic? And, you know, my colleagues like Luis León and Lara Medina look at scholars of theology and religious studies and reply, "Are you crazy? How could it not be Catholic?" People in Mexico, the United States, and throughout Latin America and the Caribbean literally use, you know, the prayer, the Lord's Prayer. It's got a crucifix, it's got a particular kind of crucifix because that's what makes it Catholic, right, to have that corporeal body of Jesus on the cross; that's going to make it Catholic compared to any other denomination.

But when you don't understand, I think, a whole group of people's relationship to the divine, you can't understand their daily experiences. And that's not to say Catholics or Chicano Catholics go around thinking about what is God doing for me in this minute, or where is God, or how is—no, it's relationships with the divine that offer another kind of profound feeling. So, spiritual relationships are just like that. And so if you're going to interview people and try to understand their domestic life or their health, those things are infused with notions of the spiritual.

NORIEGA: And how does oral history get at that? I mean, it seems like there's a border line at some point, then, between what people can say about their lives or will say about their lives and what you are interpreting from a variety of sources. So you have that thirteen-year-old girl. "Why do you still have that necklace around your neck?" What if she can't tell you? What is it that oral history is trying to pull out, in some sense, and how might it be different from some other source?

DAVALOS: Well, see this is where I don't want to split the methods, you know. At the very beginning of the interview, we talked about training, and I use the multiple tools at hand. So in terms of faith practices, you have to see the practice in action. You've got to live it with the people you're interviewing, or it's you watching a video that they have, and you dialog with them. There's many ways to do this, because you can't romanticize the methods. If you are participating in the Via Crucis in any city, you're only seeing what your eyeballs can see. You need a team of people to gather information about an elaborate ritual or procession—someone at the beginning of the crowd of 10,000 and someone at the end, the people in the middle and people watching the presentation itself and people watching the preparation. You can't be everything and everywhere at once. That's multisite ethnography for one event, right? You know, people use multisite to talk about research in two cities or two locations. No, you can't capture it only with an interview, but if you're going to try to understand their spirituality then it does require the reflective mode and you don't get the reflective mode in the moment of the event. You don't get the reflective mode as they're practicing the Posadas. You get the reflective mode through oral history, and it's when you take them through—and this is what I learned doing deliberate oral histories over and over for the Latino Art Survey. When you take them through the moments of time they start to engage the reflective mind, and that lends itself to these spiritual conversations. So even doing interviews with artists, talking about art and their life—all of this will involve conversations about the divine.

BARNETT: Did you deliberately introduce that as well?

DAVALOS: Well, it's one of the questions in the Latino Art Survey. What we had determined with the team is "Let's ask about their spirituality." And they all wanted the disclaimer—you know, fifteen Chicano artists from Los Angeles and one from the Bay Area, and they all wanted the disclaimer, "Oh, my family is not religious." [*laughter*] I'm asking about how the artist thought about God or any great being. "Did you have that training?" "Oh, yes, absolutely. God was watching you. God was caring for us." And those little *consejos*, those lessons that an elder person, usually a woman, would pass on. I forgot what the beginning question was. . . . "Would you have a special method?" Oral history, unlike a good directed interview or open-ended interview, the oral history method is what I'm saying lends itself to the reflective voice—the contemplative, the reconsidering—and that spills into the spiritual life.

NORIEGA: I think with that we can say the title of your talk will be, "Oh, my family is not religious."

DAVALOS: Yes.

NORIEGA: An interview with Karen Mary Davalos. So, thank you. [*laughter*]

Recording a Queer Community
An Interview with Horacio N. Roque Ramírez

Conducted by Teresa Barnett, June 2009

BARNETT: All right, Horacio, let's just start by talking a little about how you got into oral history in the first place.

ROQUE RAMÍREZ: Great.

BARNETT: This is kind of strange, isn't it?

ROQUE RAMÍREZ: It is. You know, it's very weird to be interviewing an oral historian.

BARNETT: And to be on the other end of it, yeah.

ROQUE RAMÍREZ: But it's good. It's a good trick to play on us, I think. [*laughter*]

BARNETT: Exactly. It reminds us of what you go through on the other end of it.

ROQUE RAMÍREZ: Exactly. You know, it had to do essentially with my own coming out, which I don't call—I don't use those terms. And now that I've been a professional gay man for almost two decades, I tell my students I get paid to be gay. They don't even know what it means. They think I'm a hooker or something. [*laughter*] I tell them, "No, no, no. I got hired to do gay studies." Basically, the way that I phrase it is, I stopped repressing my sexuality in 1991 when I was twenty-one, a fourth-year student here at UCLA. I was a political activist, a Latino immigrant, so recognizing a sexual identity, sexual consciousness, got tacked onto the other political issues. This was good and bad, because it took me years to realize I had to deal with my own individual psychological/psychic issues around being gay.

But essentially I think at that moment I realized I also liked history. I had taken a couple of courses with the late professor E. Bradford Burns on history here, and he just kicked ass. He was an amazing professor, committed, just fabulous. Later on I realized he was gay too, of course, and I thought, "Okay, that kind of makes sense." But, again, you don't have to be gay to be fabulous. But he made history really come alive, and so at some point I put two and two together and said, "Well, there's got to be gay history. There's got to be some gay Latino history."

And 1991 was the moment also when we had still a lot of death from AIDS, so it was—I've written a little bit about this—it was a very surreal, almost, I think, sexual consciousness. Because you come out but you come into a category of being at risk for death, and literally that's what it was. And so it was a very nervous identity. And of course you go through all of that and safer sex and all of that and dating, and immediately I got into what is called serial monogamy, because those things are supposed to protect you. Not necessarily. And later, I got into HIV and AIDS prevention work.

Eventually, I ended up in San Francisco, because all queer people end up in San Francisco, for better or worse. [laughter] And that's where I realized, "There's got to be some gay history here." There were some connections that I made in L.A. with some of the early history, and so I realized, "I want to do this. I want to do recording." I had read very little if anything on oral history methods, ethics, politics. I had taken a graduate seminar at Berkeley with a professor, Julia Curry-Rodríguez, and her course was on immigration and oral history methods, and it was perfect. And in the beginning, it was only HIV and AIDS, but then later on I realized it was a much larger project. So that's really where it started. Highly personal, about survival, about life and death, and pretty much fit into what they called the archival impulse, to record. Not just to fill the archive or make the archive more complete but to recognize that there are a lot of bodies missing from that archive, and if somebody didn't begin to do some recording, those voices basically would not be there. You know? For a lot of scholars and folks, that seems so simplistic. I think there's still some very profound politics about that, about having voices, and I'm glad that I did it. A lot of the people—I'm not sure a lot, but at least a few of the people that I interviewed have passed on, and so I'm glad that I got to meet them and I got to record them. So that's where it started, really.

BARNETT: You said it started with HIV and AIDS, but then it became bigger than that. How did that transition become evident to you? Why?

ROQUE RAMÍREZ: Berkeley had what was then called a Chicano/Latino Policy Project. I think now it's the Latino Policy Research something. And they had a mini-grant program, $500, I forget what it was. But hey, any money, any money counts, right? Enough to get a recorder, some tapes, some batteries. And it had to be around policy, so the policy angle for me that I could justify was HIV and AIDS. I was already meeting some of the activists in their forties, some of the so-called elders. I was in my early twenties, so to meet the gay Chicano/Latino men in their forties was somewhat odd, believe it or not.

I got the money, and I started doing very focused interviews around HIV and AIDS, but I cheated from the beginning. You know, I was all about the life history method. The very well-orchestrated questionnaire, all of this stuff, it just wasn't working. And especially the most vocal narrators, they were always tracing back and back and back. And then I realized, this is definitely a bigger project that began in the context of HIV and AIDS and death but that also wanted to capture some more of the life and some of the excitement and the pre-AIDS gay liberation zest. A lot of that sexuality and sensuality and celebration. I mean, many of those narrators, many of them activists, realized that AIDS put such a stop to liberation politics. Some people would say it put a stop to this kind of crazy sexuality perhaps too, but I think they wanted to remember how exciting it was to politicize sexuality and gender identity and how successful they had become, especially for a community of color, for Chicanos and Latinos.

Specifically my focus has been on the Bay Area, but considering migrations, including from other countries, it's really a larger project. So it began with HIV and AIDS and an immediate need to document, but it grew. It grew because while I was listening to the stories of how they got into HIV and AIDS, I realized that I could not understand the role of these activists and community educators who had come to HIV and AIDS if I didn't understand the role of AIDS and activism in their individual lives.

BARNETT: What did you find to be the particular challenges of the project as you went along?

ROQUE RAMÍREZ: Years later, upon listening to the recordings, my ignorance I think, number one. My own discomfort with sexuality. Again, I had quote-unquote "come out" at twenty-one. I was doing this project three years later, kind of a quick catch-up—a little bit too quick, you know. [*laughter*] It doesn't come that easy, I think.

BARNETT: Yeah, yeah.

ROQUE RAMÍREZ: Dealing with my own gender. I happened to land at a great moment for me, I feel. There was a queer Latino renaissance through this amazing organization that doesn't exist anymore [Proyecto ContraSIDA Por Vida], and that's a whole other story. But they were a very sex-positive, multigender, women-men agency. But that really helped me stay alive; it helped me explore. I was very shy, I was very conservative in many ways, I think. And so upon listening to the recordings I realized, "Oh my God, I can't believe I asked that," or "I can't believe I didn't ask that." Or the apparent discomfort I had interviewing somebody living with AIDS, for example. So if there is not as much explicitly sexual content or analysis in my oral histories, it may not be because of the narrators. It's probably from me, you know? And because I was relatively young, interviewing people who typically were older, there was a lot of respect that I felt I needed to pay. But the other side of that is you're not pushing, you're not being pushy enough. So my later interviews are definitely a lot more democratic exchanges in terms of venturing into community and politics and deeper issues. In the beginning, it was tamer, I think. So definitely, the preparation that I had as an oral historian was a hindrance in that I just was not as ready as I wish I was. Still, I got it done, okay?

Something I realized is that not everyone really cared about the project the way I did, and that was shocking. You know, I'm like, "Give me more!" Like, "This is history." You know, "Your life matters." Sure, but they didn't necessarily see it the way that I did, and so some of the interviews were kind of sedate in that sense and I think maybe even frustrating in that I felt that this was a critical moment and we needed to capture it, but the narrator didn't necessarily think so. Some of them thought they were doing me a favor. "Let me get this kid off my back who says he's from Berkeley and is doing this project." For some it was like, "I'm so glad you're doing this. Keep going." So you got all of that. Sexuality, of course, it's such a touchy subject. But I think I had made good connections in the community in terms of some of the gatekeepers. I was an outsider, and I later realized that that actually helped me, because I had not been involved in any of the internal drama that had happened years prior. I didn't have a sexual history with any of these folks. That actually made me somebody who could play different cards to get into these exchanges, you know? So there was that, too.

BARNETT: But you were also an insider in the sense that you were another queer man.

ROQUE RAMÍREZ: Totally. Totally. And something that I've also just realized, you know, fully bilingual. Fully bilingual, but socialized, Chicano-ized in L.A. I was eleven when I came from El Salvador, so I'm very good about Spanglish and linguistic code switching. And those skills, not all of us have them. And so I was able to interview quite a lot of people in whatever form they chose, and some people really appreciated that. There was no need for translation in any way. I had to translate it for an English-reading audience, of course, for the book. So I was an insider in many ways, in the good ways, I think, and I was an outsider in this geographic/political way, which I think was a good combination to get the project going.

BARNETT: Were there any things that you felt you weren't privy to as an outsider that it would have helped to—

ROQUE RAMÍREZ: Not everything was recorded. Not everything got on the tape. And of course I had less trust from women than from men. In terms of LGBT, the B is almost entirely missing. There's only one narrator who identifies as bisexual, a woman.

Because I was an outsider, not everyone trusted me to the same degree. And because HIV and AIDS was about survival, right, and the politics of survival and organizing and activism around life and death really, the people that I first interviewed or first contacted were those who, to some degree, had been involved in anything related to that. This is pretty much a story about activism and people organizing for their lives or for the lives of others. So that's important, I think, because this is a particular community narrative, self-selected to a large degree, a very intelligent one too and one that's very self-reflective. And again, back to my ignorance: I was way behind, interviewing some of these folks, because some of them had been doing and thinking gender and sexuality and desire for decades. I had just started, so I was just like, "God, what am I trying to do here?" I could have just turned it on and let them ramble, right? I didn't do that. But later on I realized that some of them just didn't see me as really being smart enough yet or sharp enough or, I think, critical enough. Being from Berkeley maybe gave me a couple of bonus points, but not that many, because it was not about that. People were kind to me, I think. A lot of people were kind to me, and I think the urgency of the moment, also.

There was also just no documentation. I mean, they held the documents too, so I couldn't go to the Chicano Studies Library at Berkeley, or the Ethnic Studies Library now, and say, "Let me see the special collections on Chicana lesbians." No such thing. Or "Gay Chicanos, pre-AIDS." No such thing. So in a way there was no other alternative but to really venture and dare, despite my ignorance, to engage them. And once I engaged them and some trust was gained, then the archive started popping out. And I realized, "Okay, finally we're doing something here." So yeah, there were a lot of things I wasn't privy to, I think, because I was young.

BARNETT: Yeah, yeah, that's found in any interview project.

ROQUE RAMÍREZ: I was young in terms of queer age, yeah.

BARNETT: Well, but as you said, you were an insider in some very important ways. And one thing I wanted to talk a little about is the fact that you're interviewing at the intersection of two communities: the queer community and the Latina/Latino community. And I wondered what particular challenges you saw in that, in interviewing LGBT people in the Latino/Latina community.

ROQUE RAMÍREZ: I had a huge advantage in coming from a nonreligious family—except for the cultural remnants of Catholicism that are more cultural than spiritual, okay, to make that silly differentiation. I come from a very loving family. My father just turned ninety-two a couple of days ago. I remember him making great jokes about nuns, and priests, right? My mother is a worker. That's her identity. She's always been a worker. I think the only time she hasn't worked is when she was recuperating from surgery, preventive surgery for, I think, uterine cancer, which runs in her side of the family. My father is the true intellectual of the family. He never went beyond second grade, but he's a self-taught man. And no religion. There was no time for religion; there was no interest in religion. There was no dependence on religion whatsoever. I organized my First Communion partly because I was bored, you know, and I tagged along behind a second cousin to go to church, but it really didn't mean anything. It was just the party. So religion had no place in my family, which means there was no self-hate based on heaven and hell issues.

So I had no questions of shame around religion. I had questions of shame around family. It took me a long time to tell my parents outright that I was gay—everybody knew already. I mean, I was about to file my dissertation, right? I'm speaking around the country already about the

137

work, and I'm like, "Come on, stop being such chicken shit about this." So I had cultural issues, a stigma in that sense, but not religious issues. And so again, these were activists overwhelmingly—not everyone, but a lot of them. And it doesn't mean that some of them did not have questions of shame that they had worked through themselves. But, as ignorant as I may have been about my own sexual consciousness, I was pretty secure in it. So there was no doubt. You know, "Am I this?" "Am I this?" No. It was like, "Oh," you know, "why do I look at guys on the street?" So actually the first person I came out to was my then girlfriend at UCLA. [*laughter*]

My priority was the gay Latino/Chicano community. There was no question. I went a couple of times to the Gay and Lesbian Historical Society [GLBT Historical Society] in San Francisco. They have done amazing work to this day. I try to support them whenever I can. But the few times that I went, I realized Chicanos and Latinos were just not there. I think now it's both ways. I think if any of them had tried to come to the Latino community—maybe they did—they would have gotten roadblocks. And I think the Anglo and Latino gay communities just didn't see each other basically. So I partied and socialized in the Castro District a little bit, but my priority was Chicano/Latino. I think the fact that I didn't have so much shame—a lot of which of course comes around religion, though not completely—I think that helped me deal with that intersection.

And then again, I landed in what would be probably the third generation of gay Chicano/Latino activism in San Francisco—the first one being with the Gay Latino Alliance, the second one being, with the first one, organized around HIV and AIDS, most of whom died. And then I would say the third generation is where I landed. So these folks, they had their stuff together. They knew, and there were connections to those two prior generations. So even though libraries, archives didn't quite see them or see us yet, they had been seeing themselves for several decades already. I don't know if that makes sense. That cross-generational intersection was—I want to say almost that you don't even see the intersection because you live it. It's like once you start learning this language, like "intersection of" theory, you're like, "Oh, okay, that." Well, yeah, no duh. You know, that's what it is.

BARNETT: That's just where people are. They don't perceive themselves—

ROQUE RAMÍREZ: But it's a very important question you ask. Because I realize now when I teach my classes, when I teach huge introductory classes, that Chicano/Latinos, a lot of them still just have a hard time seeing the queer, and vice versa. The queer mainstream, even though the Latino and the Chicana may be there, they still don't care to see how that intersection matters, that it's something different from a white mainstream or "the L word" or whatever it may be, right? So it's a lot of hard work. It's a lot of hard work for those who are not at an intersection. I think for me the best writing on this has been done by Cherríe L. Moraga, who's always writing from experience. And again, back to experience, you know? Whether it's around poverty, mixed race, whether you may be able to pass as white but knowing that you're not just white. Once you allow people the opportunity to see an intersection they themselves experience, right, an intersection of this empowering or empowerment. Some intersections are quite nice. If I were a wealthy gay white man who came from wealth, that's not a bad one. You know, the gay stuff may mess you up, but the wealth might help you a lot. So intersections are all over us. I think it's making them explicit and making and seeing their distinct levels of power differentials. How do they matter in the world? And I think, again, it was a total insiderness here. So we may not agree on everything, but I think I could understand what Chicana lesbians were talking about. I couldn't live it, but I think I could begin to understand it.

BARNETT: You talk about the extent to which you could understand women or not, or bisexuals. What about transgender people? That wasn't something that was necessarily on the radar when you started doing this book. We weren't yet putting a T in LGBT regularly.

ROQUE RAMÍREZ: You know, my friend Ricardo A. Bracho calls me a linguistic nationalist, because it was Spanish, Spanish, Spanish! And that was my immigrant reaction to English-based Chicano politics. MEChA [Movimiento Estudiantil Chicano de Aztlán, an undergraduate student organization] here on campus at UCLA was quite reactionary at that time. Even though we partied together, when it came down to politics, I had my identity pretty much set as a Salvadoran immigrant by then. So the first activism or organizing work that I did around gay Latino identity was in Spanish. We were nationalists with a couple of friends here at UCLA and some outside who were doing a magazine, a gay Latino magazine, in Spanish. We wanted that link with Latin America, and we knew that that would prevent us from communicating with some of the English-only speaking community, and it did, of course. So we were kind of set that way. But I'm sorry, back to your question again, because I'm backtracking.

BARNETT: Well, I was just asking, transgender—

ROQUE RAMÍREZ: In gay Latino L.A., in the public life, in the social life of gay Latino L.A., drag shows are like—it's what's done. And it's not just the drag show for the sake of entertainment, although that's very much a part of it. But it's the drag queen on the street, the tranny, whatever the term may be, that gets arrested. John Rechy, who's mixed race, who wrote *City of Night*, being of Chicano and I think Irish or Scottish descent, he writes about that. He's honest about that too, that, you know: those are the first ones to get arrested, the queens, the ones in the street, the ones flaunting their queerness. And so even though the transgender term had not been as central to me yet, I knew that that was part of it. So in Proyecto ContraSIDA Por Vida, the agency where I landed in San Francisco in the mid-nineties, transgenders were very much front and center as part of the agency.

So the term *transgender* already began to have a real meaning in terms of human beings and political actors and people with social lives, full lives. And I began to respect that. I don't think I necessarily quite got it, but I was humble enough to realize, well, hell, if I felt that I had been something for twenty-one years and then realized I wasn't, well yeah, why not be able to identify that you actually belong to another sex, another gender? And I have to say, for the most part, all of the transgender women, male-to-female transgender women, Latinas and Chicanas, that I interviewed, almost all of them immigrants, they were very welcoming. They were very welcoming. There was one female-to-male transgender narrator, Chicano native, identified. And I learned along the way. When I interviewed one MTF transgender Chicana who's a lesbian, those two combos had not really been part of my knowledge. And then I realized, "Well, yeah, why not?" Again, the heterosexism, right? The assumption that a male-to-female transgender woman was—so it gets really twisted. And I realized, ugh, I felt like such a fool, because why would I assume that she would be attracted to men? You know, assumptions.

So I have to say that early on, even though I wasn't politically engaged with transgender folks, through the spectacle of the drag queen, through that central role that the shows played in gay Latino life—I mean, we laugh about it. "Oh God, do we have to go to that club?" Because, you know, it's like a one-hour drag show. "Can you put up with one hour?" We want to dance, right? And it's like "One more. Can you just do half an hour?" But it's so central, and it's something very interesting, I think.

And I haven't really written about it enough yet, but there's something very important about the role of the transgender body, specifically the transgender woman, I think, in Chicano/Latino culture. So I can say that it was tough, but it was very eye-opening. Yeah, yeah. The one narrator who was female to male, he could pass as a man easier than a male-to-female transgender woman could pass in the Latino community, everything else being equal. And of course, as he schooled me, that has to do with the aesthetics and the extremes that the Latino body has to go through to womanize herself around makeup and body shape and all of that. Men could look like anything, and you say, "Oh, that's a good-looking man." "That's a fat man." "That's a skinny man." But, you know, "That's a man, or looks like a man." So those politics are really interesting too. And I think it's in San Francisco. People always ask me, "Why don't you do a comparative study of San Francisco and L.A.?" I'm like, "Hell no. Comparative work is a lot of work. Let me get my tenure first."

And back to oral history, I think the life history approach— Again, my beginning being around HIV and AIDS, wanting to do that, and then realizing, "Oh my God, there's just so much more." You get very hungry to know more of the history. These life histories are so rich. And this is not the only community left that is rich; we know that probably every single community has very rich lives. But because we're dealing with a community of color in the U.S. where a lot of them are immigrants, many of them are undocumented, and they're queer bodies, right. There's different permutations in the lifespan that happen that really make that life a lot more complicated and exciting.

You know, I was writing another essay about the lifespan. What is the queer lifespan in 2009? Now medications basically are keeping most [HIV-positive] people alive if you have access to them and you have the regimen and all of that. The lifespan fifteen years ago for a queer man was pretty short compared to the so-called general population. That has shifted, but it has not shifted evenly for all communities. Definitely the black community has been in crisis from the very beginning, acknowledged or not. Latinos are not too far behind, although we've done better. This is why I always push for the life history approach in all my classes, because I don't want my students to just do this almost surgical digging in with questions like, "Okay, tell me what you think about migration." And that's it. And so the rest of that narrator's story is left out, which I think is a travesty, because all the ideas, all the analysis we have at a particular point in our lives are probably connected with other things. And there's just so much to be thinking about and writing about. And of course that's part of what has dragged out my book this long and why I don't have tenure yet! [*laughter*] But that's about to change.

BARNETT: But I think one of the crucial methodological points of oral history—one that people don't realize if they haven't done it—is that you gain so much from doing these life history interviews.

ROQUE RAMÍREZ: Yeah.

BARNETT: As you went along doing these life history interviews, what sort of areas did you start to explore that maybe you weren't exploring at first, or what kinds of questions might you have started to ask? You said you weren't probing enough at first.

ROQUE RAMÍREZ: One big failure, and I'm surprised no one caught it in the beginning—one narrator did, but I didn't pay enough attention: religion. Some people see me as an exception in not being religious, but I'm not sure to what degree that's true. I don't know how religious all Latinos are really, I just don't know. Religion plays no role in the book and in the writings, and I say, you know, big sorry, but I missed it. That's okay. Somebody else can do it.

I think one that was hard in the beginning was actual sex. Yeah, outright sex. And it helped that by the time I interviewed some narrators we had become friends, either through indirect work or collaborations. Because I lived in the community or close to it, I was part of it, right? So I became part of the queer Latino community. I was recognized as an activist. Also, I was recognized as someone whose activism was taking form through education, and I think those two things are not mutually exclusive. And it's frustrating—as I advise a lot of grad students now, and undergraduates, there's an assumption that the moment you get to the university, you have left the community, and your activism. I say, "No. If you do extremely well here, the community is going to benefit, and believe me, even if you want to forget, they will remind you." It's very, very frustrating.

But I think some of the people who opened themselves up in their homes felt that "Okay, he's one of us. He's one of ours, and he's doing his contribution that way. And he's still here and he's still doing his thing." You know? And sometimes I would have to hide for a couple of months. I literally had to move away from San Francisco when I realized, "There's no way in hell I'm going to finish my PhD with all the excitement going on here," where you can walk to so many places, hang out, socialize, party, and on any one night there would be three or four exhibits going on, all around gay Latino culture. It was just too much. I said, "Okay, no, I need to finish. I've got to pay the bills, too, at some point, right, pay the debt."

But the sex part: I think toward the latter half of the interviews it became a little more exciting because I was able to push the narrators to tell me more, women and men, and some of them were more forthcoming than not. But I think that also had to do with my own comfort with sex, with queer sex. A lesbian-identified narrator told me, "My fucking around on and off with a guy here or there doesn't mean that I'm not a lesbian. It just means that sometimes I just fuck around with a guy, you know, this particular guy, let's say." And guys, same thing too. So recognizing bisexual practices that don't necessarily lend themselves to bisexual identities in the open—some of that became a little more open toward the end. The narrators themselves were challenging me, you know, and this is why it's weird to be on this side. "Ask me more specific stuff. Don't ask me general stuff." It's like, "What do you want to know?" Literally, they asked me, "Well, what do you want to know?" And I'm like, "Ooh." [*laughter*] You know? So, sex and sexuality. In terms of HIV-positive gay Latino men or transgender women or men or lesbian women—actually any of the narrators really—I think very few of them actually spoke to it on tape, for a lot of obvious reasons. Creating a record of their feelings, that may be just difficult to process.

The most explicit narrator was the one that I've already written about and published, Teresita la Campesina, who was a transgender woman and a singer. She had such a public life from the beginning because she was a singer in her fifties. She had lived long enough to benefit from some of the medications that helped her, but being in her fifties, she was very open and public about living with AIDS. And she was pretty wild. She was amazing. She was someone very difficult to force to focus. For example, I have very few recollections about details of her childhood, let's say, when she was institutionalized at a state mental hospital and given shock therapy. We're talking 1950s here. She kind of went all over the place. But she was very explicit about saying that was part of her identity, being a fifty-year-old transgender woman with a talent, a singer, an amazing singer, but being very public about her status as living with AIDS too, connecting with a new generation of people. I think, literally right now as I'm speaking, I think I get it, in that she was probably afraid that a lot of us in our twenties would forget a lot of the things she and her generation had gone through. I think that's what it was. I think that was part of why she was so forceful and sometimes, you know, unethical in terms of outing other people liv-ing with HIV or AIDS. You just don't do that, right? But she wanted to make sure AIDS and living with AIDS was part of the narrative of the community and her survival.

She eventually passed away in 2002, but she was linking the genera-tions, and she was putting herself at the center, really. In many ways she was one of the best narrators and one of the most challenging because she had so much to say. What little she said in any one minute or two minutes was so thick in meaning. I'm still kind of going through all of that. One interview, I think three hours tops, that we did. But she was so committed to her story and to the story of her generation, because she was one of the few ones alive, I think. So she was great in terms of being explicit about sex. But she was also somebody who had lived through sex work and was not shy about it. She wasn't the only one. Other narrators had too, including a gay man. So I got better in terms of talking about sex.

It's good that the project took a while. In a way it was good that I stopped recording after a while, even after some people finally came out of the woodwork and said, "Okay, now I can do it." I said, "I can't, this is just—I have to stop." You know, closure. I was overwhelmed; some nights I could not fall asleep, feeling the pressures of history I felt I carried with me. I started in 1995, and I did the last interviews probably in 2003 as a postdoc, and that was it. So we're talking eight years as somebody doing this pretty much on my own, and that has its benefits and its drawbacks. I think, for example, "Wow, why didn't I do a radio show series with some of these interviews through KPFA Pacifica Radio?" But then I think, "No, this was okay." You know, this was a project. I'm going to let it sit for a while, close it, get the book out, and then think about the next one. I'm prob-ably going to end up staying in the L.A. region, Santa Barbara included. But I really have a lot of commitment to the life history project. And I think having my father being such an older person at ninety-two, and my mother's seventy-six, not far behind, that I appreciate age and aging. I appreciate it more as a gay man in the ongoing context of AIDS. We're twenty-five-years-plus into the AIDS epidemic, a crisis for many of us. Community projects take a lot of work. And faith—not the institutional kind, but the embodied kind.

BARNETT: Yes, they do.

ROQUE RAMÍREZ: Yeah.

BARNETT: So do you plan to donate this to an archive?

ROQUE RAMÍREZ: This is many things, right? So the tapes are there. The tapes could go into several different places. They definitely belong, I think, in the GLBT Historical Society of San Francisco. They definitely belong at Berkeley too. But copies can be made, too, and so I think they can go in many places. The only restrictions would be the narrators, whatever restrictions the narrators place on that. The transcripts, of course, I don't know, a whole other thing; those could land even online, and all the politics that we can get into. It's taken a long time, because I myself transcribed probably two-thirds of all these tapes. Finally, when I became a faculty member, I had some support from student research assistants.

So yeah, that's going to be the next project. But it's a lot to think about at the same time. It's a lot. This is why oral history work is just so hard. And when you're doing work in what we can refer to as, you know, intersecting identities, intersexual communities, queer-specific in my case, of color, immigrant, you're dealing with a lot of different levels of political engagement or expectations. So I was doing recording, earning trust, hanging out, taking my classes, transcribing, dealing with all the drama that is grad school at a place like Berkeley in the 1990s, when doing oral history was not—I don't think it was anything sophisticated. I don't think it was cool. It was theoretically—

BARNETT: Wasn't seen as theoretical enough.

ROQUE RAMÍREZ: Not at all, not at all. And now, I can laugh, but I feel very secure. I feel very secure in the commitment that I made, even if I did not see some of the theoretical sophistication that can come out of oral history. A lot of the writings that are so critical—[Alessandro] Portelli, [Luisa] Passerini—I could not have grasped at the moment, or that was not my priority at that moment. But doing all of that at the same time and then considering archiving it was just like, "No way. No way can I handle this right now."

BARNETT: Yes, yes, it's a whole separate thing.

ROQUE RAMÍREZ: It's just like finally somebody returned my phone call, and after the fifth, sixth try, you know, we got to record. That's what I tell my students. It sounds easy. It sounds really easy, and that's the hook of oral history, as you know. It's great because students are like, "Oh yeah, I'm just going to do an oral history." Or unfortunately, as one of my colleagues dismissively said, "Well, I'm just going to do oral histories." And it took me back and I'm like, "Wow, okay, well, try." You know?

BARNETT: Exactly, exactly.

ROQUE RAMÍREZ: And I think I'm a pretty good oral historian. I don't think I'm a great one. I think I'm a pretty good one. I think there are bad ones, and I think there are some people who shouldn't even try. You know, stick to analysis or anything else.

This project started in 1995, so it has been going quite a long time. And every time that I feel stressed about, "God, I've got to get this done," I go back to Kennedy and Davis's *Boots of Leather, Slippers of Gold*, because that was a fourteen-year project, if I'm not mistaken. It's a reminder that it takes a lot of work. And that was a team effort in many ways, with an amazing product at the end. And in terms of sex, I think that's the best, that's still the top work that we can refer anyone to in terms of being able to get sex and sexuality and desire on record through oral history methods. With a caveat that—and they tell us why in their intro—no actual names are given, and they actually use a policy that they instituted. It's been the opposite for me in that I've tried to always use actual names unless the narrator tells me not to, and the narrative suffers or not because of that decision. So I've kind of become this very rigid, strict historian. I want names. I want places.

BARNETT: "The narrative suffered or not." In what ways would it suffer?

ROQUE RAMÍREZ: Well, if I had told a narrator, "You know, we do not have to use your name, we do not have to use your birthplace"—if I had been that explicit in the beginning, it's possible I would have got more sex out of a narrative. It's most likely, yeah, I would have. But because I didn't do that, because I was going into their birth history, their family history, where were they born—I mean, they're giving me the 411 on where they come from. Chances are they're not going to tell me where they get off. So you can't get it all, I think, in this product.

BARNETT: That's always a really difficult issue, interviewing about sexual issues.

ROQUE RAMÍREZ: But that's okay. You know, I have to say, that wasn't my goal also, which is fine. My goal was not about, "What is a gay Chicano?" No. "How does a Chicana become a lesbian?" No. "What does it mean to be a transgender Mexican immigrant?" No. Not really. The project was about a community's history, its political and cultural life, its social life, in this city pretty much. So it is a San Francisco project: they're not memories of San Francisco per se, but they're memories from San Francisco. And so I have to remind myself as I finish the book that that was the goal.

I remember meeting somebody at a bar, a gay Latino guy in a Pasadena bar that's not there anymore—Encounters, I think it was called—years ago. And I started talking about my project. You know, not many people do what I do. So the people who are interested are like, "Oh, wow." So we exchange business cards or whatever, and then I send him a chapter or two or something, an article. And later on he gave me comments, saying, "I felt disappointed that it wasn't about that, it wasn't about how to explain to someone what a gay Latino is." Because it's not a psychology project in that sense, right? So those are very different projects. It's interesting what people expect. I think a lot of my students hate to go through a lot of the historical stuff I throw at them, because that's where I'm coming from. I want them to know and to be connected to roots. I don't tell them so much about the steps or the cycles or the stages. That's never been my thing, even though I was a psych undergrad major here at this place. [*laughter*]

BARNETT: I have a question on the confidentiality again.

ROQUE RAMÍREZ: Sure.

BARNETT: Were there ever times in actually writing the book where, even though you had the material, you thought, "This is something I don't want to reveal"?

ROQUE RAMÍREZ: Yes, absolutely. And sometimes a narrator, they catch it. "Well, we'll edit this out later." They say it.

BARNETT: So they review their transcripts or they review your manuscript?

ROQUE RAMÍREZ: Yeah, to whatever degree they want or they have the interest to do it, because not everyone does. I'm being very honest about that. I've sent chapters, I've sent pieces, I've sent very detailed e-mails. "Look, this is how I interpret it." Sometimes just there's no reply, and sometimes it's just, "I completely have trust in you," and then there are some who say, "Yeah, definitely, please do not out so-and-so or so-and-so." It's really complicated.

BARNETT: So it sounds like you have a real interchange back and forth through this whole writing process. It's not like you just did the interviews and that was that.

ROQUE RAMÍREZ: Oh no! Again, what's the commitment you make to the ethics, to the politics? And I'm thinking, "What is the commitment in terms of ethics and politics with a narrator who has passed on?" I think that commitment is even greater, because the dead can't talk back at you, at least not in this, you know, in this format. [*laughter*] You know, they may do something to you later on. A living narrator can sue me, can say something, whatever, right? But a dead one can't. So I have to be very careful about how I interpret. I've had a lot of exchange. E-mail helps with those who have access, but then, you know, a lot of postage, a lot of sending copies, sharing this, sharing that. And it's not that any of them have stopped publication to any degree, but they have made me think about, again, what is the point? So I have to go back. "What is the point of you wanting to reveal that? Is it really part of the central story that you want to tell?" And if it's not, cut it.

BARNETT: Have they ever disagreed with your interpretation? Not what you put in so much, but what you said about it?

ROQUE RAMÍREZ: They haven't told me, but I'm sure they do. A couple of them said I make them sound smarter than they feel they are. But I'm like, "That's not my fault. That's just how I see it." But no, no. No one has—you know, you're bound to make errors if you're not careful. I, for example, trusted a narrator's interpretation of this white politician in seventies San Francisco as being a lesbian. Truth is, the politician's never been a lesbian or lesbian-identified. Okay, major apology, major correction I have to do, right? But in terms of people telling me, "No, I think you over—" They do tell me, for their own reasons, "No, I think the story's more about this," even if it didn't get on tape. And I say, "Okay," and we will disagree about it. But it's never been so much that I have to take something back.

BARNETT: You said you owe responsibilities to the dead. That's an interesting notion. How do you work through your responsibilities to the dead? You have their material. How do you make sure you stay—

ROQUE RAMÍREZ: And they're the only ones for whom you don't need any release signatures. The dead are dead, at least that's University of Chicago policy, according to one of the assistant editors there.

BARNETT: Yeah, well, at least for publication. If you donated the interviews somewhere, you'd need somebody's signature.

ROQUE RAMÍREZ: Right, right. I just feel that because these people shared their lives with me in life and they entrusted me, to a large degree, with their story, I have a responsibility. And there's a document. It's not just me saying, "Oh, I had a story," you know, or you were half-drunk and somebody told you something. No. There's a record. I feel extra responsible to be fair and accurate to their memories. You could get it all wrong. You could manipulate, you could exploit. It happens all the time in academia. Not just in academia, but definitely in academia. I mean, people don't have to be dead to be exploited, but I think the dead are especially exploitable. And we could do that analysis of many catastrophes. You know, Auschwitz or other global crises have been exploited and remain exploitable to some degree. I think it's worth considering that. And so, again remembering that I began this project around questions of life and death, I have to take death very seriously. I'm not talking about the Holocaust. I'm not talking about indigenous peoples when the Europeans came. But I am talking about a particular kind of death that has been taking place, and so I remain very conscious about that.

One of the narrators that I write about in an essay, he was still alive and I shared the essay with him. He was extremely happy about it, took the essay back to Mexico to see if they could translate it into Spanish. He was just really proud that his life got into print through an academic medium in some way. He then died. But it was a very small part of his interview that I had used for that essay. So now that he's dead, I remember how proud he was of my first interpretation and I think, "Well, I wonder what he would think about this one now."

So I think it's just human reciprocity and the role that the scholar, that the academic, that the writer has. Because I've been burned myself. Not in horrific ways, but I think I was misinterpreted or misquoted or both in the book *Gay L.A.* by Stuart Timmons and Lillian Faderman. Stuart, I know he's been going through some very difficult times. We did an interview over the phone. But I think the way the book framed my comments is not accurate. At UC Santa Barbara, the poor students have a horrible newspaper. Ugh, the worst. They totally misquoted me when they interviewed me about one of my students who really was sex-positive, really pushing work that he was doing for the Chicano; the paper totally misinterpreted my comments. So it sucks, because you have no control over that. That's why I think the memories of the dead are precious and fragile things to be messing with, so we better be very careful about them.

149

It's hard to write about people, living or dead. It's like I'm thinking, "God, what's my next project going to be? It's probably going to be about some nineteenth-century something, you know, and maybe not about people. Maybe mountains or something." Because it's a lot of work to write about people, you know?

BARNETT: Yeah, yeah, I understand that.

ROQUE RAMÍREZ: In the meantime, I think oral history's just so exciting. We have the Oral History Association and all the conferences. They remain very nice, open spaces, and I'm still in it. Yeah, so it's been a tough, very exciting road.

BARNETT: It's exciting, but much more work, I think, than people know, and much more complicated than just going to the archive every day.

ROQUE RAMÍREZ: Or turning on the recorder. Or saying, "Well, I'm just going to do oral histories now."

BARNETT: I have two questions wrapping up. One is, what advice would you give people on interviewing around issues of sexuality? And the other one is how does interviewing LGBT people apply to— Sometimes people hear about interviewing in LGBT communities and say, "Well, that's good in LGBT communities," but they never think of transferring some of those kinds of questions and concerns to interviewing nominally straight people.

ROQUE RAMÍREZ: Sure.

BARNETT: And so those are my two questions. What advice would you give people interviewing about sexuality? And how does the kind of interviewing you do transfer into interviewing in communities that may not be LGBT communities?

ROQUE RAMÍREZ: On the first one, about interviewing LGBT, queer people, I think the more you know about the community, about the individual, the better. If you're talking about an eighty-year-old lesbian narrator who has had no public life, that means spending the time with her before recording. A lot of the narrators, they want to share your life. That's part of the test, right? So having coffee, having a meal, doing work sometimes for them, helping them out. That's what some people call action research. I never claimed my research was action research, but there was probably some of that in it. So just realizing that it's a big commitment you're making and you have to be there and you have to be present and you have to be giving. This is a project that I was able to do as a graduate student when I didn't have to pay my loans. I didn't have a car, no car loans, no home loans, no back taxes, none of that stuff. I could actually commit. I could actually give of myself. And that's what it takes, I think. Once you become a professional in whatever realm, life gets more complicated and taxing. So you can't do a community history project probably. You may do a neighborhood, a small one. So just being giving, I think. Knowing as much as you can. Being open. Not being afraid, also. I don't think you have to be queer to be interviewing queer people. I'm not that much of an essentialist. I think it can help. It can also be a hindrance, because you may have some assumptions about what being a lesbian is like or what being a gay man is like, or about religion, let's say.

Now, the second question is interesting in that I think you don't have to interview queer people to deal with gender and sexuality. And we shouldn't have to go to queer archives to deal with gender and sexuality—and this is back to the intersection—just as we shouldn't have to go to the Ethnic Studies Library to deal with race and ethnicity. So this is where hopefully the more intersectional work will do its magic, in that you should be able to find critical racial analyses—I think of lesbian writers of color, again Cherríe Moraga, Gloria Anzaldúa, and to some degree, Audre Lorde—deep racial analyses of the United States through lesbian experiences, profound stuff. And the other way is you should be able to have some deep gender and sexual analyses from Chicano and black archives, and I think we do have some of those too. I think of the late Marlon Riggs, filmmaker, amazing gay black man who died of AIDS. He worked in both spaces really, really well.

But you don't have to go to queerness to be able to deal with gender and sexuality, and that means that we need to be more critical of ethnic studies scholarship. Very, very few, maybe just one or two books that I know of are explicit about the sexuality of the people they interview or even thought about it. With everybody else, silence creates the assumption of heterosexuality. Right? And that's horrible, because then people have to come to me or take my classes, and then I become the queer. You know, "Oh, talk to Horacio." Well, no. Again, another colleague said, "Well, why do we have a class on gender?"—meaning one of the big intro ones. "That's essentially a class only women can teach." I'm like, "Duh! That's exactly the problem, mister. You know, you should be reading about gender and women and sexuality." So that's really hard.

151

I'm not sure how effective I've been in my teaching in that my work outs me, so I think already people come to me because of queerness. But I want them to come and talk to me also about questions of immigration, okay, and racism, right? When I breathe "the R word" in queer spaces, silence. I'm like, "What's up? Why can't you deal with this shit?" And vice versa. In nonacademic spaces where people don't know me, once I bring sexuality into the picture, people get uncomfortable and say, "What? You know, this is a Latino space."

So that's a lot of hard work, but I think queer scholars, we're doing the work because we're committed to it. And most of us, we're queer scholars, but we need to challenge the ethnic studies canons and not be afraid to deal with gender and sexuality. And the next generations of scholars, my grad students, I think they know that and it's great to see that. And no apologies, which is great. And I think it has to do with the fact that the space has been created in Chicano and Latino studies in terms of opening up more racial analyses and queer history. It's a long way to go. It's been a lonely road, let me tell you. It's like I have benefited from it because I am the one queer Latino community historian on the map as far as I know. The only other one, I think, would have been Yolanda Retter Vargas, who passed away, who wasn't in academia per se but was a librarian. But that's it. So when they need a panel and they want to add the basic food groups, I count as one or two. So great, I get invited to a lot of places. And the same thing on the Latino side. When the more conscious Chicano/Latino scholars want to have some queerness, "Oh, where's Horacio? What's he doing that weekend?" [*Laughter*]

BARNETT: Just the spice on both sides of the —

ROQUE RAMÍREZ: You know, it hit me a couple of years ago. I realized, "Of course," and I'm like, "That's okay." Obviously it's benefited me to some degree. It's been a mutual use, to put it that way. But it's hard.

And I need to be hard on my students about needing to know your history. If you're going to do a queer project, you need to know the history and you need to do it and ground it. You have to ground it. And, more and more, stuff that is purely theoretical, I just won't do it. I won't support it. I won't advise, because I'm again back to step one. The archival impulse, the documentary impulse, it matters. I think, you know, oral history and history still matters.

Contributors

TERESA BARNETT is the head of the UCLA Library's Center for Oral History Research. She has been in the field of oral history for more than twenty years, during which time she has overseen interview projects in a wide variety of areas and has conducted numerous oral history workshops and classes. In addition to administering the Center for Oral History Research, she is an adjunct faculty member in UCLA's Department of Information Studies and has served as oral history editor of the *Public Historian* and book review editor of the *Oral History Review*.

KAREN MARY DAVALOS is chair and professor of Chicana/o studies at Loyola Marymount University in Los Angeles. Her research interests encompass representational practices, including art exhibition and collection; vernacular performance; spirituality; feminist scholarship and epistemologies; and oral history. Her book *Yolanda M. López* (UCLA Chicano Studies Research Center Press, 2008), volume 2 in the A Ver: Revisioning Art History series, was distinguished with an Honorable Mention at the 2010 NACCS Book Awards and the 2009 International Latino Book Awards. She is also the author of "The Mexican Museum of San Francisco: A Brief History with an Interpretive Analysis," in *The Mexican Museum of San Francisco Papers, 1971–2006* (UCLA Chicano Studies Research Center Press, 2010), which received Second Place for Reference Books in English at the 2011 International Latino Book Awards. Other publications include *Exhibiting Mestizaje: Mexican (American) Museums in the Diaspora* (Albuquerque: University of New Mexico Press, 2001), and the second edition of The Chicano Studies Reader: An Anthology of Aztlán Scholarship, 1970–2010 (UCLA Chicano Studies Research Center Press, 2001), which she co-edited. Davalos is past lead editor and managing editor of *Chicana/ Latina Studies: The Journal of Mujeres Activas en Letras y Cambio Social*.

FELICIA SCHANCHE HODGE holds a joint position as professor of nursing and public health at UCLA. A member of the Wailaki tribe in Northern California, Hodge received her master's and doctoral degrees from UC Berkeley. She taught and worked at the University of Hawaii, UC San Francisco/Berkeley, and the University of Minnesota prior to coming to UCLA. She is currently the director of the CAIIRE research center (Center for American Indian/Indigenous Research and Education) and is past-chair of the American Indian Studies Interdisciplinary Studies Program. Her research for the past thirty-five years has been on behavior change in the area of cancer control and chronic health conditions among American Indians and indigenous populations. Dr. Hodge has led major grants in tobacco control, diabetes, cancer screening, nutrition, and pain management. She has developed and tested the talking circle intervention and storytelling data collection methodology.

KAREN L. ISHIZUKA is an independent writer and former documentary producer. She is the author of *Lost and Found: Reclaiming the Japanese American Incarceration* (University of Illinois Press, 2006) and several articles in anthologies and journals and the co-editor of *Mining the Home Movie: Excavations in Histories and Memories* (University of California Press, 2007). Her documentary work based on life histories includes *A Song for Ourselves* (2009), *Pilgrimage* (2007), *Toyo Miyatake: Infinite Shades of Grey* (2001), *From Bullets to Ballots* (1997), and *Looking Like the Enemy* (1995), all directed by Robert A. Nakamura. She has been a Getty Visiting Scholar in Residence, has served on the National Film Preservation Board, and has curated *America's Concentration Camps* for the Japanese American National Museum. Her awards include an HBO Producers Award; First Place, C.L.R. James Scholar Essay; and three CINE Golden Eagles. She is currently writing *Making Asian America*, which will be published by Verso Press in 2013, and completing a PhD in anthropology at UCLA.

NANCY RAQUEL MIRABAL is an associate professor of Latina/o studies at San Francisco State University, where she specializes in oral history and theory, Latina/o histories, and Afro-Latina/o diasporas in the United States. She is currently a 2012–13 Scholar in Residence at the Schomburg Center for Research in Black Culture, where she is completing a manuscript titled "Hemispheric Notions: Diaspora, Masculinity, and the Racial Politics of Cubanidad, 1823–1945," which will be published by the New York University Press. She has collaborated with Diana Lachantanere and Pamela Sporn in completing an oral history of Melba Alvarado, which will be archived at the Schomburg Center. Recent publications include "Melba Alvarado, El Club Cubano Inter-Americano, and the Creation of Afro Cubanidades in New York City," in *The Afro-Latina/o Reader* (Duke

University Press, 2010); "Displaced Geographies: Latina/os, Oral History, and the Politics of Gentrification in San Francisco's Mission District," in *The Public Historian* (2009); and "Dyasporic Appetites and Longings: An Interview with Edwidge Danticat," in *Callaloo: A Journal of African Diaspora Arts and Letters* (2007). Dr. Mirabal is also the lead editor of *Technofuturos: Critical Interventions in Latina/o Studies*, and she serves on the editorial board for the *Latino Studies Journal, Oral History Review*, and *Phoebe: Journal of Gender and Cultural Critique*

ROBERT A. NAKAMURA is a professor emeritus of UCLA, having taught in the Departments of Asian American Studies and Film, Television, and Digital Media in addition to being associate director of the Asian American Studies Center. A pioneering Asian American filmmaker, he has directed over twenty videos and films that have garnered over sixty awards, including several selected for the Sundance Film Festival, the Yamagata International Film Festival, and Robert Flaherty Seminar for Independent Film and Cinema. He founded Visual Communications, the oldest continuing Asian American media center in the country, the Japanese American National Museum's Frank H. Watase Media Arts Center, the UCLA Center for EthnoCommunications, and the Downtown Community Media Center. His honors include the Ann C. Rosenfield Distinguished Community Partnership Prize; Distinguished Artist, C.O.L.A. (City of Los Angeles); and the UCLA Endowed Chair in Japanese American Studies. His early work has been selected for retrospectives of the documentary form by Los Angeles Filmforum, Oakland Museum of Modern Art, and Long Beach Museum of Art.

CHON A. NORIEGA is director of the UCLA Chicano Studies Research Center and professor in the UCLA Department of Film, Television, and Digital Media. He is author of *Shot in America: Television, the State, and the Rise of Chicano Cinema* (University of Minnesota, 2000), co-author of *Phantom Sightings: Art After the Chicano Movement* (LACMA/California, 2008) and co-editor of *L.A. Xicano* (CSRC Press, 2011). He is editor of nine other books and three book series. Since 1996 he has been editor of *Aztlán: A Journal of Chicano Studies*. He co-curated four interrelated exhibitions on Chicano art from 1945 through 1980 that were on display at three art museums in Los Angeles from October 2011 through February 2012. His awards include the Getty Postdoctoral Fellowship in the History of Art, the Rockefeller Foundation Film/Video/Multimedia

Fellowship, and the Ann C. Rosenfield Distinguished Community Partnership Prize.

HORACIO N. ROQUE RAMÍREZ is associate professor of Chicana and Chicano studies at the University of California, Santa Barbara. This interview explores his oral history work with LGBT Latinas and Latinos in San Francisco. A book based on that work, *Queer Latino San Francisco: An Oral History, 1960s–1990s* is forthcoming as part of the Palgrave Studies in Oral History series. Roque Ramírez is also the co-editor of *Bodies of Evidence: The Practice of Queer Oral History* (Oxford University Press, 2012).

SUSAN D. ROSE is Charles A. Dana professor of sociology and director of the Community Studies Center at Dickinson College. The Community Studies Center directs a number of Mosaic projects that integrate collaborative, interdisciplinary, and community-based oral history projects across the curriculum. Dr. Rose uses a comparative (cross-cultural and historical) approach to the study of family, gender and sexuality, religion, migration, and violence. She has conducted fieldwork in the United States, Guatemala, the Philippines, and South Korea on evangelical movements; in Cameroon, Venezuela, the Netherlands, and Denmark on gender violence; and in Argentina and Mexico on (im)migration. This work has resulted in numerous articles, books, and documentary films. Rose is a recipient of the Michael Harrington Distinguished Teaching Award from the National Poverty Forum and the National Oral History Post-Secondary Distinguished Teaching Award.

IRUM SHIEKH has been involved in various social justice projects throughout the world. She has produced a series of documentaries that highlight the social struggles of marginal populations, such as Japanese-Peruvians interned in the United States during World War II and Indonesian Muslim women living in a matrilineal society. Her book *Detained without Cause* (MacMillan Palgrave, 2011) features narratives of six immigrants who were wrongfully arrested in connection with the 9/11 attacks and later deported for minor immigration or criminal charges. Dr. Shiekh received her PhD from the University of California, Berkeley. She currently is teaching in the Department of Ethnic Studies at the University of Oregon, Eugene.

Index